Routledge Library Editions

EARLY BRITISH ECONOMICS

I0888069

ECONOMICS

HISTORY OF ECONOMIC THOUGHT
In 23 Volumes

I	A Select Bibliography of Modern Economic Theory	*Batson*
II	Early British Economics	*Beer*
III	Nassau Senior	*Bowley*
IV	The Theory of Marginal Value	*Birck*
V	Ricardo and the Theory of Value Distribution and Growth	*Caravale & Tosato*
VI	Productive Labour and Effective Demand	*Coontz*
VII	London Essays in Economics	*Gregory & Dalton*
VIII	Capitalism and the Historians	*Hayek*
IX	The Origins of Scientific Economics	*Letwin*
X	The Individual in Society	*Macfie*
XI	Essays on Hayek	*Machlup*
XII	The Economics of Physiocracy	*Meek*
XIII	Karl Marx	*Mehring*
XIV	Marx's Critique of Political Economy I	*Oakley*
XV	Marx's Critique of Political Economy II	*Oakley*
XVI	J R McCulloch	*O'Brien*
XVII	A Key to Ricardo	*St Clair*
XVIII	Roads to Freedom	*Streissler*
XIX	Economics in the Twentieth Century	*Suranyi-Unger*
XX	Elements of Pure Economics	*Walras*
XXI	The Common Sense of Political Economy I	*Wicksteed*
XXII	The Common Sense of Political Economy II	*Wicksteed*
XXIII	Social Economics	*von Wieser*

EARLY BRITISH ECONOMICS

From the 13th to the Middle of the 18th Century

M BEER

Routledge
Taylor & Francis Group
LONDON AND NEW YORK

First published in 1938

Reprinted in 2003 by
Routledge
2 Park Square, Milton Park, Abingdon, Oxon, OX14 4RN
or
270 Madison Avenue, New York, NY 10016

First issued in paperback 2010

Routledge is an imprint of the Taylor & Francis Group

British Library Cataloguing in Publication Data
A CIP catalogue record for this book
is available from the British Library

Early British Economics
ISBN 978-0-415-31322-3 (hbk)
ISBN 978-0-415-60714-8 (pbk)
ISBN 978-0-415-31320-9 (set)

Miniset: History of Economic Thought

Series: Routledge Library Editions – Economics

EARLY BRITISH ECONOMICS

from the
XIIIth to the middle of the
XVIIIth century

BY

M. BEER

Author of "A History of British Socialism,"
etc.

"There is nothing which requires more to be illustrated by Philosophy than trade does"—
Samuel Johnson

Routledge
Taylor & Francis Group
LONDON AND NEW YORK

FIRST PUBLISHED IN 1938

INTRODUCTION

Of books which describe the commercial and industrial history of Britain there is no end; their title-pages alone would fill a fair-sized catalogue. The present book is not intended to swell their number. Its subject matter is not the growth of British trade, but economic thought, which was bequeathed to us by men of the British Isles from the thirteenth to the middle of the eighteenth century. Its primary object is to give in a concise form a connected and consecutive outline of the economic and ethical problems raised by social developments and changes, as well as of the reasonings about them and the doctrines formulated by schoolmen, city merchants, economic writers, and philosophers in the five or six centuries in question.

Vast and various is the series of folios, discourses, "conceipts," and tracts which those men were able to leave to posterity. It has been beyond my power to summarize and appraise them all. I have confined myself to giving the essentials of those works that contain some original thought or which exerted a considerable influence on their contemporaries.

It was my main effort to organize the existing doctrinal material of early British economics—first, by dividing it, according to time and contents, into consecutive periods; second, by classifying the reasonings and concepts of each period; lastly, by putting each group of reasonings and concepts, as well as its leading exponents, in their historical setting. How far I have succeeded in that attempt, is for my readers to say.

There are in these pages some fundamental views which are likely, I think, to arouse opposition and controversy, for they run counter, or will be regarded as a challenge, to accepted views concerning medieval economic legislation, the significance of mercantilism, the political and social meaning of the balance of trade doctrine, and allied topics. I can only say that my views are not the result of mere preconceptions. I did not bring them with me when I started writing, but they grew upon me in the course of my work, and I only adopted them after many searchings of heart, when I saw that they were capable of throwing light on early British economics, and of giving logical coherence and historical sequence to a series of facts and doctrines of the period in question.

There will probably be some readers who, in the course of studying these pages, will feel impelled to resist or reject those views. May I ask them to suspend judgment till they reach the final chapter? If then they fail to be converted, they will at least be rewarded for their patience by having to make up their minds to re-examine the views they had formed from former studies on the subject.

* * *

The present book is in the nature of a pioneering venture. It has the failings, but also, I hope, the strength and searching spirit of the pioneer. There are, of course, many essays, tracts, and books of all sizes which deal with various periods and aspects of early British economics, but none, I believe, with the subject as a whole.

Let me enumerate some of them. The place of honour must be assigned to John R. McCulloch's "Introductory

Discourse" to his edition of Adam Smith's *Wealth of Nations* (1828). Though it owes much to Dugald Stewart's economic researches, it is none the less a masterly performance. It exceeds in historical value his *Literature of Political Economy* (1845), which is but an extension of the *Bibliographie Raisonnée*, appended by the great French economic historian, Adolphe Blanqui, to his *Histoire de l'Economie Politique en Europe* (1837). Next in importance are the lectures delivered by Travers Twiss at Oxford in 1846, and published under the title *Views of the Progress of Political Economy* (1847). He acknowledges his obligation to McCulloch and Adolphe Blanqui. Only the first two lectures are given to English economics—the first, in particular, to an analysis of that famous tract which is now known as John Hales's *Discourse on the Commonweal of this Realm of England.* Twiss is distinguished by keen analytical power and sound judgment. I ought now—on the score of chronology—to mention Professor Richard Jones's paper "Primitive Political Economy" (*Edinburgh Review*, April 1847). He wrote, however, not as a historian, but as a free-trade agitator, who, with the peal of the Peelite joy-bells in his ears, was burying and damning everything that medieval lawgivers enacted, and all but everything that mercantilist writers reasoned concerning trade and commerce.

During the following half-century, British writers were indifferent to early economics. Only McCulloch published, in 1856, on behalf of the Political Economy Club[1] a

[1] The Political Economy Club was founded in 1821 as the result of meetings held at Ricardo's house in the preceding year.

The original members were—David Ricardo, James Mill, George Grote, T. R. Malthus, J. R. McCulloch.

selection of economic tracts embracing the years 1620–1701. The interest in such writings was so weak that only one hundred copies were printed. On the other hand, the interest in that subject gradually awakened in foreign countries. In 1857, Professor Roscher (Leipzig) published his treatise, *Zur Geschichte der englischen Volkswirtschafts-Lehre*, and in 1876, Professor Yanshull (Moscow) published the first part of a treatise on early mercantilist writers in England. Roscher compensated for the paucity of his available sources by his vast historical knowledge of economics and his trained judgment. Yanshull's treatise—written in the Russian language, of which I am ignorant—I only know from the many quotations from it given by E. von Heyking in his *Zur Geschichte der Handelsbilanz-Theorie* (1879). The latter is a slender tract of ninety pages, yet it exerted a decisive influence on economic historians who wrote in the 'eighties of the last century. Professor Schmoller's views on Mercantilism as the economic expression of the formation of national states in early modern times, have much in common with those of Heyking.

It is owing to this revived interest in mercantilism, which however is but a part—though a very important part—of early British economics, that Professor Hewins published a fragmentary outline of it in the Introduction to his lectures on *English Trade and Finance in the XVII Century* (1892) and a similar paper in *Palgrave's Dictionary*. These papers, in conjunction with Professor Ashley's endeavours to spread Schmoller's views in English-speaking countries, contributed to a renascence of early economic studies, all the more so as the theory of free trade was visibly losing its glamour. In the last few years three voluminous works on mercantilist economics have been published—Professor Elie Heckscher's *Mercantilism* (London), Professor Jacob Viner's *English Theories of Foreign Trade before Adam Smith* (Chicago University), E. A. J. Johnson's *Predecessors of Adam Smith* (Cornell University), and there is a doctoral thesis by Suviranta, *The Theory of the Balance of Trade* (Helsingfors).

Those are all studies concerning some parts of early British economics, but not embracing the whole of the subject.

* * *

During my researches I received much assistance from Professor R. H. Tawney, but I alone am responsible for the use made of it or for the shortcomings of the book.

My hearty thanks are due and gladly given to Dr. Thomas Jones and Sir Richard Rees, Bt., whose lively interest in my work was a great encouragement to me.

The suggestion to undertake the writing of a history of British economics was made to me years ago by Professor H. J. Laski. Many adverse circumstances, not unconnected with the post-war European turmoil, militated against starting on such a tremendous task, and even now, while living securely in London, I could only carry out a minor part of that suggestion. Meanwhile, one grows much older, and the infirmities of age find less resistance, the post-war years having counted double or treble their length in the life of Eastern and Central-European Jews.

M. BEER

CONTENTS

I

THE SCHOOLMEN AND THEIR PROBLEMS

1. *Beginning of Scholasticism in the British Isles*

In the three or four centuries of European turmoil and darkness following the disintegration of the Roman Empire, the embers of the holy fire of Latin and Christian learning were gathered in the seventh century by St. Isidore of Seville (Hispalis) in his *Etymologia* and *Sententiae*, and were kept burning by scholarly monks and theologians in Ireland and pre-Norman England. Three names stand out among the teachers in the British Isles—Bede, Alcuin, and John Scotus Erigena. Bede, who owed much to Irish teachers, was one of the founders of medieval theology; Alcuin, a pupil at the Church School at York (founded by Egbert, a pupil of Bede), spread the light in Charlemagne's Empire; Erigena, whom King Alfred brought over to England, enriched Latin-Christian learning by philosophical speculations derived from the Greek Fathers and mystics. The British schools in early medieval times were full of promise. They might have risen to the height which those of France and Italy reached in the eleventh, twelfth, and thirteenth centuries, if the Danish invasions had not interrupted and set back the development of the British Isles. Grievous as was the material havoc which the Danish wars wrought, the loss to learning was by far more baneful. The Danish spoliations of the monasteries and churches in Ireland and England extinguished scholarship in pre-Norman England. Erigena and King Alfred were the last flickers of early British learning and love of education.

Then followed two centuries of spiritual and moral decline of priests and monks, until the Norman Conquest brought England again into contact with Latin-Christian civilization, partly through the Archbishops Lanfranc and Anselm, and partly through English students, such as John of Salisbury, who sought learning in French schools. They sowed the seed of scholasticism and science in England, to which her great sons, Robert Grossteste, Alexander of Hales, Roger Bacon, Ricardus de Media Villa, Duns Scotus, William of Ockham, and John Wycliffe made at least as great contributions as any of the leading schoolmen in France or Italy.

Christianity, in passing from the Judaeo-Christian communities to the Hellenic and Roman world, underwent a transformation. With the Jews of old, whose minds were grounded in the Bible and in God's wonders that had occurred in the past and would occur in the future, faith was above and beyond all reasoning. The view that the existence of God stood in need of being proved by reasoning was not only arrogantly blasphemous, but as arrantly foolish as the need, at noontide, for a proof that the sun was shining. When the Jew looked for signs and wonders, it was not to prove God, but to probe whether a new prophet was truly sent from God. It was different in the Hellenic and Roman worlds, where the thinking minds looked for a philosophy, for reasoned wisdom. Or in the words of St. Paul, "The Jews require a sign, the

Greeks seek after wisdom" (1 Cor. 1, 22). The educated Greeks and Romans, who in the course of the first five centuries joined the Church, were grounded in logic and trained in dialectic, in the Organon of Aristotle and the Isagog of Porphyry, either in the original Greek or in the Latin translations and commentaries of Boethius. Their first urge, when they had adopted the new faith, was to argue about its doctrines according to the methods of the academies. Probably but few of these neophytes renounced questionings and attained to the pure faith which can only be reached through the gateway of spiritual humility.

Besides logic and dialectic, the educated Christian Greeks or Romans brought with them the ethics of the Stoics, based on the Law of Nature and all that it implied. They looked wistfully back to the primitive society bathed in the rays of the golden age and governed by immanent divine law or right reason: equality and liberty of men, common possession of the earth and the fullness thereof. They were averse to the artificial order of civilized life, with its cupidity, its lust for wealth and power, its trade and commerce, its many inventions. A similar thought is expressed in Ecclesiastes (7, 29): "God hath made man upright, but they have sought out many inventions." The Stoic views of society were, by means of interpretation, easily brought into harmony with the Biblical story of the pristine state of Adam in the Garden of Eden or with the community of goods among the first Jewish-Christians in Jerusalem (Acts 4, 32). All the Greek and Latin Fathers adhered in principle to the Stoic view that by the Law of God and Nature all was common to all and only by avarice and usurpation, or by man-made law, was the division of things, *meum* and *tuum*, constituted. The Italian monk Gratian, who in the twelfth century made a compilation of the Canon Law, did no more than summarizing the views of the Fathers concerning property. "Jure divino omnia sunt communia omnibus; jur vero constitutionis hoc meum, illud alterius est. Divinum jus in scripturis habemus; humanum jus in legibus regum. . . . Communis enim usus omnium, quae sunt in hoc mundo, omnibus esse hominibus debuit. Sed per iniquitatem . . . inter mortales facta divisio est."[1] Even in pre-Norman times those views of the Fathers were known in the British Isles. Erigena, the most learned and profound theologian, interpreted the Biblical story of Adam as symbolizing the blissful state of Nature, which man lost through cupidity, and which will be ultimately restored by God creating a new heaven and a new earth, as prophesied in Revelation (21, 1).[2]

2. *Commerce and Ethics*

Some of the Fathers looked upon commerce as sinful, or as easily conducive to sin and therefore disreputable. Many disputations were argued out on this head, in which the English schoolmen, Alexander of Hales, Ricardus de Media Villa, Duns Scotus, and Ockham took a prominent part. Even as late as in the year 1078 a Roman Council, presided over by Gregory VII, promulgated Canons, the fifth of which declared that whereas soldiers and

[1] *Decretum Gratiani*, pars prima, distinctio VIII, causa I; pars secunda, causa XII, questio I, c. 2, gloss *a*.

[2] John Scotus Erigena, *De divisione Naturae*, book 5, c. 2, 19.

merchants could not carry on their trade without sin, there was no salvation for them unless they turned to other occupations.[1]

A sin more heinous than commerce was money-lending on interest. All payments in excess of the principal were usury and against the Law of God and Nature (quidquid sorti accedit usura est).[2] The prohibition of usury was known in Anglo-Saxon times. King Alfred in his Laws (37) took it from the Bible (Exod. 22, 25), and in the Laws of Edward the Confessor (leges, 37) usury is branded as the *radix omnium malorum;* no usurer should be permitted to reside in England. Moreover, profit in commercial transactions was regarded to be no better than usury. Surplus value or the obtaining for a commodity of more than its normal market price or just price, is called by the Canonists turpe lucrum, dishonest gain. Turpe lucrum sequitur, qui minus emit, ut plus vendat.[3] A dishonest gain results from buying cheap in order to sell dear. Exchanges must be on the basis of equal values, and sales at "just prices."

The whole body of Patristic and Canonist views and Latin-Christian learning, to which Aristotle's *Ethics* and *Politics* were soon added as among the authoritative sources, was brought over to England in the twelfth and thirteenth centuries from the schools of Normandy (Bec, Caen, Avranches) and France (Laon, Paris, Chartres). The English monks and clerics adopted Graeco-Roman logic and dialectic, the study and exercise of which appear

[1] Mansi, *Collectio Sanctorum Conciliorum*, tom. 20, p. 510.

[2] *Decretum Gratiani*, pars secunda, causa XIV, questio III.

[3] *Ibid.*, pars secunda, causa XIV, questio III, c. 1, 2, 3, 4, questio IV, c. 9.

to have been carried on with great zeal at the time of Lanfranc, who was famous as the most formidable dialectician and theologian of the century. His students must have somehow overdone it, for the complaint was made that at every possible and impossible occasion they were vomiting dialectic by the mouthful: *Ubique inflati buccis Dialecticam ructabant.*[1] The students learnt much more, however, than merely disputing. *The Elucidarium sive Dialogus*, sometimes ascribed to Lanfranc, and which Giles included in his edition of the *Patres Ecclesiae Anglicanae*, contains also, as H. W. C. Davis summarizes it, some "reflections on practical morality, in which the legend of the golden age and the stoic praise of Nature is blended with the ideas of St. Benedict. . . . Few knights are good, for they are wont to live on plunder and clothe themselves with rapine. There is little hope for the merchant, for nearly all his wealth comes through deceit and perjury. . . . But tillers of the soil are for the most part saved, inasmuch as they lead the simple life."[2] This is quite in the spirit of the Fathers and Canonists, and the same views are to be found also in John of Salisbury, one of the earliest English scholars in the reign of Stephen. The love of wealth and possessions, he declares, is even worse than Epicureanism, since the passion it excites is the more violent. Avarice is the lust to get something which one does not possess and to hold fast what one possesses. Property chains man to worldly things and makes him insatiable. The soul is of so noble

[1] Quoted by Hasse in *Anselm von Canterbury*, vol. i, p. 38, footnote 2.

[2] H. W. C. Davis, *England under the Normans and the Angevins*, 1918, pp. 49–50.

and fine a nature that earthly possessions cannot satisfy it, and that it languishes if it cannot raise itself to God.[1]

3. *Growth of Trade and Commerce*

The schools of England established in the reign of William Rufus and the first Angevin kings assimilated the Patristic views on property, trade and commerce, money, interest, and profit, but must have soon found them to be irreconcilable with the ruling conditions. For, as documentary evidence shows, those were centuries of the growth of towns and the rise of the Third Estate, that is the trade and money economy. Whatever the origin and structure of towns, there can be no doubt that trade was one of their characteristics, which marked them off from the countryside. Doomsday Book mentions eighty-two towns, many of them probably no more than large villages, but they must all have had some local trading, while towns like London, York, Chester, Bristol, Winchester, Dover, Sandwich, Norwich, Lincoln, had commercial intercourse with the Norman possessions in France, with Germany, the Scandinavian countries, Flanders, and Italy. England exported wool, woolfells, lead, tin, jet, salted fish and meat, and imported wine, furs, cloth, and some luxuries. Contemporary writers, such as William Fitz-Stephen (one of the biographers of Becket) and William of Malmesbury, are full of praise of the trade, prosperity, and skill of London merchants. Fitz-Stephen relates that London, one of the noblest and most famous cities, is visited by merchants from all parts

[1] John of Salisbury, *Polycratius*, book 7, ch. 16, also book 6, ch. 5.

of the world, who send there the most various wares. The Arabs send gold, Sabeans spices and incense, Scythians arms, Babylonians palm oil, Egyptians precious stones, Syrians purple vestments, Gauls wine, Norwegians and Russians furs.[1] William of Malmesbury writes in a similar strain of the works and wealth of the London merchants and of their commercial transactions with the traders of the whole earth.[2] In the twelfth and thirteenth centuries many towns received royal charters. Several of them had weavers' gilds, and also a gild-merchant to regulate trade.

The importance attached to foreign trade may be seen from Magna Charta, which in Section 41 guarantees to "all merchants safe and secure exit from, and entry to, England, with the rights to tarry there and to move about by land as well as by water, for buying and selling according to ancient and right customs, quit from all evil tolls (*sine omnibus malis toltis*), except when such merchants, in time of war, are of the land which is at war with us. . . ." Fifty years later, that is, in 1265, the representatives of 166 cities and boroughs made their first entrance into Parliament. The Third Estate was politically recognized.

It is not our purpose here to outline the development of trade and commerce in England in the twelfth and thirteenth centuries, but rather to bring out the salient points of that development, in order to realize the growing divergence between the trend of Patristic and Canonist

[1] William Fitz-Stephen, *Vita St. Thomae* (Prologus) in Giles, *Patres, Ecclesiae Anglicanae*, pp. 174–177.

[2] William of Malmesbury, *De Gestis Pontif. Angl.* Liber II (beginning); Migne, *Patrologia*, tome 179–180, p. 1514.

doctrine in the schools and that of the economic realities which were developing in the towns. That doctrine would have been much more congenial to the first centuries of the Anglo-Saxon period, when economic life was still primitive, that is, more of a tribal kind, with its natural economy. In the Norman and Angevin period the doctrine grew manifestly out of tune with the prevailing state of things.

4. *Conflict between Ethics and Economics*

That was the problem of the English schoolmen. The doctrine, based on irrefragable authorities, could not be abrogated, but neither could the stubborn economic facts be gainsaid. They had to be reconciled with the assistance of logic and dialectic, as St. Augustine had tried to do eight or nine centuries before, when Patristic doctrine impinged upon Roman money economy, under which absolute property, trade and commerce, interest on loans, buying cheap and selling dear, that is, making profit on sales, were lawful and regarded as natural. The attempts at reconciliation made by St. Augustine[1] were now to be followed up and carried to a satisfactory conclusion by the schoolmen, when the revived towns of Western and Central Europe had submerged tribalism and embarked upon a commercial economy.

[1] Enarratio in psalmum 70, chapter 17, contains St. Augustine's main arguments concerning lawful and unlawful trading as well as concerning gain on sales. The passage is much quoted by the schoolmen and all theological writers when treating the question of commerce and profit. A good popular example is the recital of the merchant in Aelfric's *Colloquium*, which is true both to the letter and the spirit of St. Augustine's merchant.

The English schoolmen who resolved the contradictions between doctrine and facts were Alexander of Hales, Ricardus de Media Villa, Duns Scotus, and in some parts William of Ockham (Occam), all Minorites and advanced thinkers, who adjusted Patristic and Canonist principles to the advancing economic life, thus clearing the way for mercantilism, though this work constituted only a minor part of their task. They regarded it as their main business to support and strengthen by reasoning the established tenets of faith or dogmas, to which they devoted the bulk of their voluminous writings. In these matters no deviation was admissible. On the other hand, the doctrines concerning economic life were stretched, interpreted, or supplemented to fit the economic realities, though the schoolmen believed that they were but fulfilling the law of God and the teaching of their saintly predecessors.

The starting-points of the schoolmen are authoritative texts, either from the Old and New Testament, or from the Fathers, such as Ambrose, Augustine, Chrysostom, Cassiodor, or from the works of later authorities, such as Isidore of Seville (*d.* 636)[1] and particularly Peter Lombard (*d.* 1164), whose *Quatuor Libri Sententiarum* (written about 1150 or ten years after Gratian's *Decretum* and consisted in a compilation of all the theological learning of the Fathers and Canonists), became the textbook for theo-

[1] "St. Isidore of Seville (writes William of Malmesbury) was so celebrated for learning and sanctity that in our time (that is the twelfth century) Adolfonsus, King of Gallicia, purchased his remains for their weight in gold and had them conveyed from Seville to Toledo" (*Chronicle of the Kings of England*, Giles' translation, London, 1847, p. 173).

logical students and was much discussed in the universities and commented upon by the schoolmen.[1]

Since the twelfth century Aristotle as author of the *Politics* and *Ethics* grew in authority equal to that of the Fathers.[2] He was alluded to as the "Philosopher," without his name being mentioned.

The established tenets of faith and all theological metaphysics are outside the scope of our work. We shall confine ourselves to the economic and social doctrines, in so far as they are dealt with by the English schoolmen. Alexander of Hales will be treated in greater detail and largely in his own words, for, as it will be seen, a fairly good knowledge of one leading schoolman forms the best introduction to the study of the others. They all follow the same methods, have the same ends in view and appeal to the same authorities, differing only in subordinate points or in emphasis on certain aspects and amplifications of the matters they argue about in "distinctiones" and "questiones" according to the economic circumstances of their time or the influence which they had undergone.

[1] A good introduction to Peter Lombard's *Sententiae* is to be found in J. de Ghellincks's *Le movement théologique au XII. siècle*, Paris-Louvain, 1914.

[2] Filmer in his *Observations upon Aristotle's Politics* (p. 1) wittily remarks, "What cannot be found in Scripture, many do look for it in Aristotle."—Francis Bacon relates that it was said by many concerning the Canons of the Council of Trent, "We are beholden to Aristotle for many articles of our faith."

II

ALEXANDER OF HALES (ALENSIS)[1]

1. *Community and Private Property*

In his *Summa* (pars III, questio 27, membrum 4, art. 3) Hales alludes to Isidore's definition of the Law of Nature[2] which also contains the words *communis omnium possessio*, and he asks, Is by the Law of Nature everything common? It seems not. First, we see everywhere acquisition and restitution of things which belong to others. From this we may infer that there is private property. Moreover, Isidore's definition itself admits the acquisition of things that may be captured in the air, on the earth and in the water, as well as the restitution of loaned goods.[2] There is thus by the Law of Nature

[1] Alexander of Hales was born in the last quarter of the twelfth century in Gloucestershire, probably in the Manor of Hayles, and died in Paris in 1245. He belonged to the Order of the Minorites and was famous as "Doctor Irrefragibilis" on account of his *Universae Theologiae Summa*, which was held in high esteem by the Pope, but was adversely criticized by Roger Bacon. It may be remarked that in the year of Hales's death the Abbey of Hayles (Glos.) was founded. Whether this foundation had for its purpose to commemorate the great schoolman and Minorite or it was a mere coincidence, is not known.

[2] St. Isidore of Seville, *Etymologia*, book V, chapter 4, treats of Law of Nature and defines it as follows:

"Ius Naturale is common to all nations and contains everything that is known to man by natural instinct and not by constitution and man-made-law, and that is, the joining together of man and woman, procreation and education of children, *communis omnium possessio et omnium una libertas*, the acquisition of things that may be captured in the air, on the earth and in the water, restitution of loaned and entrusted goods, finally, self-defence by force against violence."

property, and therefore not everything is common. Secondly, theft is against the Law of Nature[1] for the appropriation of other people's property is against divine law. Property, therefore, is a Law of Nature.

Opposed to that view, we find in St. Augustine (in Johannem, ch. 2) that it is only by man-made law that we say this estate is mine, this slave is mine, this house is mine; cancel that law, who could then say this estate is mine, this slave is mine, this house is mine? From this we infer that property is only made legitimate by positive (civil) law, and therefore that the appropriation of things that are common is against the Law of Nature.

Regarding the inference that he who appropriated common things commits a sin, it must be pointed out that "common" has two meanings. First, we call common what belongs to nobody, and this may be appropriated. Secondly, "common" is something which belongs to the community, such as highways and common lands. These things must not be appropriated, because such an appropriation is an injury to all.

With regard to Isidore's definition *omnium una libertas*, it is clear that slavery is against the Law of Nature. God made all equal.

Solution.—There are various considerations as to the community of things. We must consider things from the point of view of necessity, goodness, and equity. First, in a state of general need—an emergency—everything must be common and distributed to all; this applied to

[1] The schoolmen considered the Decalogue to be the essence of the Law of Nature. Seeing, then, that a commandment against theft was necessary, property must have existed in the state of nature.

things that are necessary for the sustenance of man. . . . Secondly, one must consider a state of things which is good. In the state of uncorrupted nature everything is common; conversely, in a state of corrupted nature it is good to possess certain things as property, else the honest man would suffer privation, while the dishonest would ravish everything, and the world could not exist. We thus see that in certain circumstances the Law of Nature demands community, and in others private property. Finally, from the point of view of equity, certain things cannot be appropriated, such as air and sea; but things which can be turned into property and are still in nobody's dominion, should be assigned to those who first occupy them.

2. *Trade and Commerce*

In *Summa* (pars III, questio 50, membrum 1) Hales puts the question, Is commerce lawful? *Utrum negotiato sit licita?* He replies by referring to Chrysostom, who points out that the Lord Jesus ejected the buyers and sellers from the Temple, by which action Jesus implied that a merchant can never please God, and that a Christian, therefore, may not be a merchant. Chrysostom further declares that a Christian who desires to be a merchant should not be allowed into the Church, for it is said in Psalm 70 (71), 15, "Because I don't know trading (*negotiationem*) I shall enter into the glory of the Lord." He continues by saying: I shall show who cannot be called a merchant and who can be called so. He who buys a thing and transforms it, that is, he buys it as raw material to be worked up into a useful thing, such a man is not a merchant. For instance, if one buys timber for the purpose of making a box, or sheets of paper to write a book, such a one is not a merchant. But, he who buys a thing and leaves it whole and unchanged, only to sell it at a profit, such a man is a merchant and cannot be allowed to enter into God's temple. Since, however, nearly all business activities belong to that category, a Christian must avoid trading.

Also Cassiodor alludes to that passage in Psalm 70 (71), 15, "Because I don't know the books (*litteraturam*)[1] I shall enter into the glory of God," and asks, "Is commerce then anything else but buying cheap and selling dear?" And he continues, saying, "Such merchants the Lord ejected from the Temple, with the words, Ye make it a den of robbers."[2]

In opposition to that, we read in St. Augustine, "Lechery is always prohibited, but commerce is sometimes lawful and sometimes not." St. Augustine on that passage in Psalm 70, 15, "Because I don't know trading" (*negotiationem*) says, "it may be argued that Christians should not

[1] The translation of Psalm 70, 15, is, as we may have noticed, not uniform. Some of the Fathers write, "Because I don't know trading" (*negotiationem*) and some, among them Jerome in the Vulgate, write *litteraturam* instead of *negotiationem*. The Hebrew word in question is *sphorot*. No explanation is given for the two Latin variants. St. Augustine (Enarratio in Psalmum 70, chapter 19) draws attention to those variants and finds it difficult to account for them and remarks, "ubi alii habent *negotiationem* ibi alii *litteraturam*." I venture to offer the following explanation. The Hebrew term in question in psalm 70, 15, is *sphorot*, which means books or writings; maybe that some manuscripts had *skhorot*, which means merchandise. The variant would thus involve one letter only, but giving two different meanings.

[2] Cf. *Decr. Grat.*, distinctio 88, causa 11, Palea *Eicens*.

engage in commerce," but the merchant replies, "I am procuring and bringing goods from far-off countries. I am simply trying to get wages for my labour, and the labourer is worthy of his hire. From this it follows that I can rightly sell dearer than the price which I gave." St. Augustine continues as follows: "I do not approve of covetous traders, since the covetous blasphemes when he is losing and tells lies for the sake of gain; but those failings are in the man and not in his trade, which can be carried on honestly. In all vocations, be it in those of shoemaking, tailoring, farming, sins are committed, but it is not the vocations which are at fault, it is the man who sins. From this it follows that trade and commerce are lawful, provided they are carried on without lying and without perjury. There can be honest traders as there are honest farmers. . . . The Philosopher says that since everybody needs many things which he cannot himself produce for his sustenance, such as food, garments, housing, etc., man must live in society, that is, with other men of various vocations, and they form a trading association, in which their members exchange to their mutual benefit their goods and services. . . . Trade and commerce are thus not an evil, but in accordance with the Law of Nature. And, when Cassiodor says that trading is illicit because it means buying cheap and selling dear, this can only apply to traders who are buying up all the goods necessary for sustenance, such as corn, in order to make them scarce and then sell them at prices arbitrarily fixed. Such traders shall be ejected from the Church and all holy places."

Solution.—The question as to whether trading is licit

or illicit must be considered from the point of view of the person, the thing, the mode, the time, and locality. Trading is illicit when it involves actions that are in themselves evil, such as fornication and usury, but trading is in itself not evil; it becomes evil if pursued by persons who are forbidden to engage in trading, such as clergymen. Trading is illicit if pursued for sinful purposes, such as forestalling. It is forbidden in times that ought to be devoted to divine service and prayer, such as Sundays and Festivals. It is forbidden when carried on in a locality consecrated to the service of the Lord, such as Churches, and it was for that reason that the Lord ejected the merchants from the Temple. Trade is lawful when pursued honestly for the purpose of supplying our fellow-man with the goods he needs; it is lawful when pursued to obtain the wherewithal to help our fellow-men in need; it is lawful when the merchant brings from other lands the goods necessary for sustenance and preserves them from deterioration, larceny or fire; his travels and stewardship are labour and the labourer is worthy of his hire.

Trading, then, is licit because in harmony with the Law of Nature, unless carried on from the mere lust of gain and to the injury of society. Moreover, not only is trade and commerce lawful, but so also is the earning of a moderate gain, provided that the merchant transported the goods from another place to the market or to his store, where the consumers can obtain them. Hales thus amplifies the opinion of Chrysostom by adopting the argument of the merchant to whom St. Augustine alludes. While Chrysostom thinks trade lawful when it is combined with transforming the commodity, Alensis regards also transport as labour, and makes lawful not only trade and commerce, but profits derived from them. Through transport—and there is no trade or commerce without transport—trading rises to the dignity of labour, which, according to the schoolman, is the rightful source from which to earn one's sustenance. Hence, the merchant is entitled to sell his goods at a higher price than he gave for them, and the gain which he thus procures for himself is not turpe lucrum, but wages of his labour and industry.

3. *Aristotle and the Schoolmen on Money*

Before reproducing the views of Hales or of any other schoolman on usury, a few preliminary observations on money may be necessary, for we are now approaching the most difficult part of the schoolmen's economic and legal dialectic. Unless we can fully enter into their conception of money, we shall hardly be able to follow their arguments, and all scholastic reasoning on usury may appear to the modern mind as little better than sophistry.

As in all other matters of faith and life, the schoolmen started from authoritative texts, and proceeded to fortify or amplify them by logic. The texts onusury are clear enough. They are to be found in the Old Testament (Exod. 22, 25, and Deut. 23, 19), which prohibited the Hebrews from lending money or victuals to their kinsmen on usury; but those laws were not absolute, for they permitted interest on loans advanced to non-Jews. The Fathers, however, considered that the prophets and Jesus made the prohibition of usury general, and they refer to Psalm 15, 5, Ezekiel 18, 8, and Luke 6, 35, where it is said, "Lend, hoping for nothing," which is interpreted as a command not to hope for interest or any other material advantage. These views have their origin in Jewish and primitive Christian social morality, and would be quite satisfactory if economic development had not increasingly advanced on proprietary and commercial lines, which made loans a normal part of economic life. Usury grew into a theological problem, which had to be solved by reasoning and interpretation.

The schoolmen in the thirteenth century, with Alexander of Hales at the head, adhered to the theory of Aristotle that money was nothing else but a measure of value or price.[1] This theory maintains that, just as a yardstick measures the length of a piece of cloth, or an imperial gallon measures the cubic capacity of a vessel, or an avoirdupois pound measures the weight of a commodity, so money measures the price of objects of commerce. Here and there, it is true, we perceive in scholastic literature a flash of light on the substance or intrinsic worth of money; but the view of money as exclusively a measure of price remained uppermost, as we must remember that money and value and price are the most intricate subjects of economics. Sir William Petty, in the second half of the seventeenth century, could still speak of "the deep ocean of all the mysteries concerning money,"[2] and money has remained to this day a problem that is puzzling and troubling humanity.

The schoolmen found for their theory of money the

[1] The whole problem of the Aristotelian economics is fully dealt with in the last section of this book, pp. 228–234.

[2] Sir William Petty, *Economic Writings*, ed. Hull, vol. i, p. 85.

authority of Aristotle, whose fame in medieval times far transcended that of his own age in ancient Hellas, though his reasoning about money is for the modern mind very difficult to follow. In *Politics* (1, 3, §§ 6–21) he writes as follows: "When the inhabitants of one country became more dependent on those of another . . . money necessarily came into use. For the various necessaries of life are not easily carried about and hence man agreed to employ in their dealings something which was of some use . . . for example, iron, silver, etc. Of this the value was at first measured by size and weight, but in the course of time they put a stamp upon it to save the trouble of weighing and marking the value." He then goes on to declare that, after the invention of coin, retail trade developed into money-making and riches were identified with a hoard of coin. Wealth is assumed by many to be only a quantity of coin, "while others maintain that coined money is a mere sham, and nothing by nature, but entirely by convention, for when it is called in or displaced by another commodity as a medium it is worth nothing. And indeed he who is rich in coin may often be in want of food, like Midas in the fable." Aristotle adopts the view of the conventional nature of money, as is evident from his *Ethics* (book V, 3–8), where he deals with the subject in connection with commercial intercourse. Money, he declares, has not a natural but a conventional existence. *Nomisma* (money) derives its validity from *nomos* (the law). It was invented for the purpose of measuring the value of things and making them comparable when being exchanged against one another. It shows, for instance, how many pairs of shoes or quantities of produce are the equivalents of a house. "Money, then, is like a measure that equates things by making them commensurable." It thus makes exchange possible, and hence also association, for without exchange there could be no association.

Money, being only a medium or a conventional token used for the purpose of indicating the equivalents of a number of commodities which are to be exchanged against one another, is a barren thing. (I may remark that Aristotle does not use the term "barren," he only implies that the Greek term for interest—*tokos* which means offspring—cannot properly be applied to money.) It is, therefore, unnatural to use it for money-making, that is, for lending it on usury. "The sort (of money-making) most hated and with greatest reason, is usury." For money is intended to be used in exchange, but not to increase at interest.

Aristotle's theory of money offers great difficulties to our understanding. So keen, disciplined, and logical a thinker, who sifted and tested his views and who observed life and gathered experience in the whole Hellenic world, must have had cogent reasons for his views—reasons which are still unknown to us. Maybe, in the course of these studies, which will often touch upon the problem of money, I shall be more able to enter into the mental atmosphere in which Aristotle worked, and to point out how he arrived at his conclusions. Meanwhile, I only venture to say that his views would rather correspond to a state of society in which the production of goods is still far from adequate to the daily needs. In an economically advanced society, where supply responds to demand, money reveals its true nature as the most convenient commodity, which, so to speak, can at a moment's notice be transformed into any other desirable commodity. Still, the double aspect of money, that is, its function as a stamped medium of exchange and its intrinsic commodity value, gave rise to much confusion, since man is apt to mistake the outward appearance for the essence of reality. The civil lawyers and schoolmen, based on Aristotle, formulated the rule "Nummus non est à natura, sed à lege."[1] The confusion became worse confounded through the debasement, deterioration and clipping of the coinage which went on in mediaeval and early modern times, and which caused appearance and reality, denomination and intrinsic value, more and more to diverge.

The schoolmen, while pleased to be able to lean on so great an authority as Aristotle, were sometimes more enlightened, for some of them knew that money is not sterile and does breed money when applied to productive labour. But, as regards commercial transactions and loans, they shared the opinion of Aristotle that money was not more than a statutory measure of prices. Just as an imperial gallon was intended to measure the cubic capacity of a vessel, a yardstick to measure the length of a piece of cloth or timber, an avoirdupois pound to measure the weight of bread or meat, so was money intended to measure the price of things in buying and selling. Hence it follows that, since it would be wicked to demand interest, say a yardstick and a half, from a neighbour when lending him a yardstick, which he would

[1] "Denarius vocatur numisma, nomos enim lex est . . . Denarius non est mensura per naturam, sed *nomo*, id est à lege." (Thomas Aquinas, *Comment. in Ethic. Aristotelis*, liber V, lectio 9, sub b.c. f.)

return as soon as done with, so it is wicked to demand an increase say, £150, from a neighbour when lending him £100, which he will return in a certain time. A yardstick, an Imperial gallon, an avoirdupois pound, a sum of money, they are one and all merely statutory contrivances for measuring and weighing. In this sense, money is barren and does not breed money, any more than a yardstick breeds yardsticks.[1]

4. *Usury*

Hales, who, as pointed out in a former chapter, gathered together all the arguments to render trade and commerce legitimate, was one of the first schoolmen who broke through the law of usury by introducing the titulus morae (compensation to the creditor to be paid by the debtor for delay), notwithstanding his marshalling all authorities and arguments against usury. In his *Summa* (pars. III, questio 36, membrum 4; likewise questio 50, membrum 3) Hales states that according to divine and natural laws usury is prohibited. We read in Luke 6, Date mutuum nihil inde sperantes. To obtain something over and above the principal is against the seventh commandment. The question is, why should a loan contract be different from a lease contract? It seems that both are similar. In both cases the owner expects to have his property returned, and something more than the capital value thereof. He who lets a house or a field is handing over his property for a certain time in order to obtain more than its capital

[1] In Shakespeare's *Merchant of Venice* (I, 3) Shylock virtually argues that money breeds money, while Antonio calls money a "barren metal."

(praeter sortem). Now, considering that a usury contract is sinful, why should a lease contract be lawful?

The answer is that the two contracts differ in several respects. First, he who owns a field obtains corn from it; he who owns a house has his shelter in it. And if the owner thereof hires it out, it is the lessee and not the owner who enjoys the usufruct, while money in possession of the owner produces no utility of its own and can only be used in exchange. Secondly, he who lets a house or a field does not hereby transfer the ownership, so that the owner has to bear all the risk which ownership implies, while in a loan (mutuum) the owner transfers the ownership (dominium) of the money to the borrower, who is then responsible for the risk (unde mutuum dicitur quasi de me tuum). Finally a house or a field deteriorates through age and use, so that the lessor receives his property back in an inferior condition, while in money there is no wear and tear, so that the creditor receives his money back in the same condition as he had given it. For all these reasons a lease agreement is lawful, and a usury contract sinful. If, however, the loan contract fixed a certain date for repayment and the debtor is unable to meet it on maturity, then the creditor is rightfully entitled to be indemnified for the delay, and such an indemnification is not usury. This is the titulus morae.[1] Alexander of Hales was not without influence on his younger contemporaries, Albertus Magnus and Thomas Aquinas.

[1] "Similiter et in mora: ut si deberes mihi centum solvere ad certum terminum: quod quia non fecisti: opportuit me illam pecuniam accipere ad usuram: tu teneris mihi restituere illam et servare indemnem. Sed planum est, quod in tali casu restituere, non est usura." (*Summa*, pars III, questio 36, membrum 4, resolutio, ad quartum, ed. Cologne, 1622, vol. ii, folio 275.)

III

RICARDUS DE MEDIA VILLA

1. *Community and Liberty*

Very few reliable data are known of the life of Ricardus de Media Villa (Richard of Middleton). The best documented are the years 1283 and 1284, in which he received his B.D. in Paris, and soon after his D.D. and D.LL. As the latter degree could only be attained at the age of thirty-five, his biographer, Edgar Hocedez,[1] surmises that he was born in 1249. He was a Minorite, and an elder contemporary, and perhaps a friend, of Duns Scotus. As to the year of his death nothing positive is known. From various allusions to Ricardus by contemporaries it is inferred that he predeceased Duns Scotus by a year or two, that is, in 1306 or 1307. Biographically he stood between Thomas Aquinas, who was his senior, and Duns Scotus, who was his junior, and both overshadowed him intellectually, though he was known as "doctor solidus et fundatissimus." He well deserved these epithets, and even something more, for he was a learned schoolman, and, considering his time—the height of mediaevalism—a very advanced thinker on economic matters.

The bulk of his published writings consists of a large commentary on Peter Lombard's *Sententiae*, and of a relatively smaller volume of *Quodlibeta*. Both works, as

[1] Edgar Hocedez, *Richard de Middleton, sa vie, ses œuvres*. Paris-Louvain, 1925.

far as economic and political matters are concerned, were written under the influence of Thomas Aquinas and Aristotle. He is of opinion that in the state of "naturae lapsae" the law of nature concerning community of goods and equal liberty ceased to be appropriate. In consequence of corrupted nature, slavery and private property are more apt to promote a peaceful and laborious life in society. In an extreme social emergency, however, individual property must give way to community of goods. Contrary to Alexander of Hales (Alensis), who thinks equal liberty for all to be an incontestable law of nature, Ricardus —in conformity with Aristotle—thinks that slavery is not unnatural. The slave, however, should not be treated as a mere chattel: the master should respect the human rights of his slave. The State, that is, the power of kings and masters, is likewise the consequence of the original *lapsus*. Princes, nevertheless, should not govern as absolute monarchs, but according to the customs, rights and the consent of the people.[1]

2. *Lawfulness of Trade and Commerce*

In the eyes of Ricardus the old question as to the lawfulness of trading was settled by St. Augustine, Alexander of Hales, and Thomas Aquinas. Trading is lawful for the following reasons. First, the different wants of men and their consequent demand for mutual services, that is, exchange; secondly, nature rightfully dictates that men in their intercourse should assist one another

[1] *Sententiae*, II, dist. 44, articulus 2, questio 1; *Sententiae* III, dist. 37, articulus 3, questio 4.

"inasmuch as they are all under one prince who is God"; thirdly, the natural endowments and products of the various countries differ in kind as well as in quantity and quality; some abound in goods in which others are deficient. It is thus natural that men should mutually exchange their superfluities and supply the deficiencies.

The real problem for Ricardus is this. The main purpose of trading is gain. If there is gain, somebody must lose, that is, the gainer is injuring his fellow-man. According to Roman law, overreaching in commerce is to a certain degree licit, but according to the Fathers and Canonists such trading is wrong, for divine and natural law dictates that there should be equality of exchanges; while Aristotle also thinks gainful trade to be unnatural. "Of the two sorts of money-making," he observes, "one is a part of household management (economic), the other is retail trade (lucrative); the former is necessary and honourable, the latter a kind of exchange that is justly censured, for it is unnatural, and a mode by which men gain from another."[1]

It is essentially a problem that engaged the thought of the Free Traders from the time of Adam Smith onwards when dealing with the well-known Mercantilist view that the gain of one is the loss of another, or as Francis Bacon expressed it, "whatsoever is somewhere gotten is somewhere lost."[2] The Free Traders attempted to show that in trade both the exporting and importing countries gain, and that therefore international trade is quite in accordance with the principle of commutative justice. Ricardo proved this by his labour-value theory,[3] but

[1] Aristotle, *Politics*, 1, 3, 8 and 9.

[2] Francis Bacon, *Essays*, 15 (On Sedition and Troubles).

[3] David Ricardo, *Principles of Political Economy*, 1817, ch. vii.

Ricardus de Media Villa, following Aristotle, regards utility as the essence of value or price, and he, none the less, succeeded in showing that in exchange both parties gain and that therefore trading is lawful though lucrative. He reasoned as follows:

"Let us envisage two countries, A and B, unequally endowed by nature. A produces corn in abundance, but little wine, while country B has an abundance of wine and a deficiency of corn. We know that the market price or the just price of a commodity varies according to its plentifulness or scarcity. The same commodity when plentiful is less appreciated than when it is scarce. In this manner a sextarium of corn in country A will be cheaper than in country B, while conversely a dolium of wine in country A will be dearer than in country B. Now, it is natural for the business of trade and commerce to equalize supply. The merchant, then, buys corn cheap in country A and sells it at the higher market price that is ruling in country B, or he buys wine cheap in country B and sells it at the higher market price that is ruling in country A, so that in reality the consumer is not in the least overcharged, for he pays for each commodity the normal price, the just price, which is ruling in his respective country. The exchanges are equal, yet the merchant earns his profit, and he does so rightfully, for, far from having injured either country, he brought benefit to both. His profit is therefore neither usury nor turpe lucrum. The same rule of equality of exchanges which we find in international trade applies also to the business transactions of individuals in their own country. The commodity which the consumer receives is of more immediate utility to him than the money he gives for it, while to the merchant the money he receives for his commodity is of greater immediate utility than the commodity which he surrenders, so that both draw equal benefits from the exchange."[1]

3. *Difference between Gain and Interest*

The question is, why gain from trade is rightful and that from a loan is sinful. "A trade agreement and a loan agreement," says Ricardus, "differ essentially from one another. In trade both parties expect gain, in a loan (mutuum) the intention of gain is prohibited, for the Gospel admonishes the lender to grant the loan without hope of gain" (Luke 6). Further, "From a sterile thing nobody can demand increase, and money is in itself a sterile thing, and it can only breed an increase through the labour and care of the man who thus uses it. Therefore, it is not the money but the man who produces the increase through his labour and industry, and since man is lord over his own labour and industry (quia homo dominus est sui laboris et industriae) the increase belongs rightfully to him and not to the lender."[2] Finally, Ricardus employs against usury the argument, elaborated by Thomas Aquinas on the basis of Roman law, that *mutuum* being a loan of consumable things the lender cannot justly demand compensation for the use of it. The meaning of that argument is this: There are commodities of which use and substance are separable—for instance, a house which the owner may continue to own while

[1] *Quodlibeta*, II, questio 23, articulus 1; *Sententiae* III, distinctio 33, articulus 3, questio 4.

[2] *Sententiae*, IV, distincto 15, questio 5, sexto queritur.

the tenant has the use of it; in such commodities the use exists apart from the substance and compensation for use is licit and is not usury. On the other hand there are commodities of which use and substance are inseparable —for instance, corn; if the owner sells or lends it, he cannot demand the price for, or the return of, its substance and, additionally, compensation for its being eaten. Money is regarded as a consumable commodity; it is consumed as soon as the exchange is effected, and as the borrower returns the money, he pays the price, so to say, for the substance. The lender has no right, therefore, to demand compensation for its use, because the use does not exist apart from the substance.

Despite all those arguments against money-making from loans, Ricardus, like his predecessors (Alensis and Aquinas), makes large concessions to the money-lender. He permits poena conventionalis (a fine paid by the debtor for not fulfilling the provisions of the agreement), likewise damnum emergens (the creditor is to be indemnified for the loss entailed in lending the money which he might have used in the meantime for the purpose of his own exchanges); further, titulus morae (indemnification for delay in repayment), and periculum sortis (indemnification for the risk of a loss of capital). With those concessions, though limited by reservations, money-lending was rendered legitimate and lucrative.[1]

Altogether, one is tempted to look upon Media Villa as an enlightened economic pioneer of urban civilization.

[1] See also Schreiber, *Volkswirtschaftliche Anschauungen der Scholastik*, Jena, 1913.

IV

JOHN DUNS SCOTUS

1. *Remarks on his Life and Work*

Known as doctor subtilis, Duns Scotus was one of the most famous schoolmen, and the originator of a school bearing his name and rivalling in influence that of Thomas Aquinas. Neither the township nor the year of his birth is known with certainty. Ireland, Scotland, and England are each laying claim to having been his native country. It is assumed that he was born about 1265 or 1266. The only biographical data beyond cavil are that he was a native of the British Isles, that he studied and taught in Oxford and Paris, was a member of the Minorite Order, and died at Cologne in 1308.

Of all his very voluminous writings, which embrace theology, metaphysics, logic and some scientific subjects, our concern is with his economic and social views, which he treated in his commentary on Peter Lombard's *Four Books of Sentences*—namely in his *Sententiae*, IV, distinctio 15, questiones 2–19, on restitution of things. The space which he allotted to those questions is, for the sociologist, like a tiny island in the midst of an agitated ocean of learning. His reasonings on them are not as coherent and closely arranged as those of some of his predecessors, but they are illuminated by original and surprisingly modern conceptions, particularly as regards political sovereignty and the formation of civil society.

His views on property are those of the schoolmen in general, but more extensively elaborated than elsewhere in scholastic writings. Scotus starts likewise from the community of goods as taught by jus naturale, then comes the fall of man and the transition to the division of things into private property through positive laws which, however, he attempts to link up with the Law of Nature. As to trade and commerce he is quite free from the Patristic and Canonist misgivings about their lawfulness. Trade and commerce are for him everyday facts and necessary activities of society, which cannot be questioned as long as they are carried on with proper regard for the welfare of all, that is, in a Christian ethical way in conformity with the golden rule, Hoc facias alii quod tibi vis fieri. For all his modernity concerning trade and commerce Scotus could not free himself from the Aristotelian and medieval concept of money as merely a measure of value, though he declares that silver is in itself a valuable metal when used for ornaments, etc.

2. *Origin of Property and State*

The division of things was not made by natural or divine law, for by natural law all is common to all, as is argued by St. Augustine on St. John, chapter 2, and quoted in Gratian's *Decretum*, distinctio 8, causa 1. By what right, asks St. Augustine in commenting on that passage, doest thou defend the possessions of the Church? By divine or human law? The divine law we have in the Holy Scripture which says that the earth and the fullness thereof are the Lord's; the human law we have in the ordinances of the kings.

There is evidently a clash between divine and human laws, for we see that the dominion over things is individual (rerum dominia sunt distincta) and there is mine and thine, this being the foundation of all institutions, by which men enter into contracts for obtaining things from others.

The reasons for this are as follows. First, the use of things, according to right reason, must serve the purpose of society, that is, to make the peaceful and concordant intercourse (pacifica et congrua conversatio) of men possible and allow them to obtain the necessary sustenance. Having that paramount social purpose in mind, we may observe that in the state of innocence, that is, before the fall of man, the community of goods served that purpose best; men did not take more than they needed, and all had their sustenance. Secondly, post lapsum that precept of the Law of Nature was revoked, because in that state the community of goods did no more serve the social purpose of peaceful intercourse, since the wicked and the covetous by using violence grasped more than they needed and thus injured and oppressed their fellow-men who could no more obtain their sustenance. Also the Philosopher in his *Politics* argues against Socrates (Plato's *Politeia*) and points out that community of goods leads not to concord but to strife. Finally, the revocation of the precept of the Law of Nature implies licence to appropriate and mark off what was common to all. From this it follows that the first division of things was not made by divine or natural law, but by some positive enactment.

Was that positive enactment just? And who gave it?

In order to enact a just law the legislator must have two

qualifications—prudence and authority. He must be guided by right reason, which dictates what is good for the community, and he must possess authority, for it is not the law by itself that holds society together, but authority which presides over it.

Before we proceed with the argument it may be useful to remark that when Scotus speaks in this connection of *auctoritas* he really means what we call sovereignty in constitutional law.

Scotus goes on to say that there are two kinds of *auctoritas*, namely, *auctoritas paterna* and *auctoritas politica*. What does he mean by auctoritas paterna? He does not use it in the sense of paternal government or absolute monarchy, which we find in Filmer's *Patriarcha*, where several passages suggest that the defender of Charles I knew the reasonings of the subtle doctor on the subject. From the definition given by Scotus, though loosely formulated, and from the whole context, it is fairly clear that of the two kinds of sovereignty one appertains to chieftainship of a tribal society, and the other to a principal or head of a civil society. He writes, "Paternal authority relates to a society (which derives from) natural descent and does not relate to the inhabitants of civil society, and the law came from living together under one father, not (existing) corporeally but mentally." This is, evidently, the legendary tribal ancestor of the kindred. And this interpretation draws strength from the definition of auctoritas politica, which forms an undeniable contrast to his definition of auctoritas paterna. Political sovereignty, says Scotus, does not relate to kinship or vicinity (nulla consanguinitate vel propinquitate), but to a group of individuals originally strangers to one another (multae gentes extranae et diversae), and obeying nobody, but voluntarily come together to form a *civitas* or a *terra* in order to preserve their peaceful existence, and by mutual consent elect a *princeps*, whom they should obey, either for a certain time or for life, or they vest sovereignty in the community itself.

Here we have the whole social contract theory, or the conception of creating civil society by individuals, kinless, free, and independent, and who voluntarily surrender their powers to an individual, whom they elect either as president or hereditary king, that is, making him their sovereign.

Those sovereignties, the paternal (or tribal) and the political (republican or monarchical), provided they are guided by right reason, may rightfully enact laws. The law given by paternal sovereignty is natural law, for by divine commandment (the fourth in the Decalogue), children are bound to obey their father. The law enacted by political sovereignty is just, for it rests on the consent of, and the election by, the people. (Auctoritas vero politica quae est supra extranaeos, sive in una persona resideat, sive in communitate, potest esse iusta ex communi consensu et electione ipsius communitatis.)

The division of the lands was made either by the auctoritas paterna, as Noah after the flood divided the lands among his sons, or it was done by mutual consent, as we read, for instance, in Genesis 13, of Abraham and Lot, the former conceding to the other that part of the land he would choose to take. Or it may have been done by some auctoritas politica, either the elected *princeps* or the community itself, who decided that all lands not occupied yet should be divided among themselves. And then they spread over the whole face of the earth, some occupying this part and others another part.[1]

3. *Trade and Commerce*

Scotus is, as mentioned before, quite free from misgivings about the lawfulness of trading, though its aim is gain. Scotus flourished at a time when foreign merchants were eagerly competing for the English staple commodities—wool, woolfells, lead, and tin—and concluded with King Edward I the Carta Mercatoria (1303). Trade is thus necessary and useful for the well-being of society. The productive capacity of the various countries and the needs of men differ in quality and quantity and can only be equalized and served by merchants. Their knowledge, industry, care, and risk, in bringing goods to the market or storing them for emergencies, entitle them to the gains on their sales. In countries with either abundance or deficiency of goods, but without merchants capable of managing foreign trade, the governments would have to engage at high salaries men who understand trade, in order to take charge of export and import.

The gain which the merchant earns is a salary, proportionate to his station in life, for the public service he renders to the country. But it must be honourable trade, carried on without fraud and at prices freely and justly agreed upon by buyer and seller, who are not all too hard upon one another. Only those merchants are vicious who

[1] *Sententiae,* IV, distinctio 15, questio 2.

neither work up nor transport or store the goods for regular trade, but forestall, regrate, and engross them in order to make supply scarce and thus raise prices above the market level.[1]

4. *Usury*

Scotus refers to the Old Testament prohibition of usury as well as to Luke 6. A loan is essentially a work of Christian compassion with one's fellow-man in need. No material gain can be expected to accrue from it. As to legal points against usury, Scotus argues mainly that a loan (mutuum) is a transfer of property from the creditor into the ownership of the borrower (*mutuum do tibi meum*); it is, therefore, unjust on the part of the creditor to demand compensation for the use of a thing which is not his. The borrower, it is true, may use the loan lucratively; it is, however, not the money that earns the surplus, but the industry of the borrower, since money is barren.

Though on the whole every additional payment over the principal is usury, there are a few cases in which an additional payment is lawful. There is the poena conventionalis, that is, a fine for the non-payment of the loan on maturity, if such a fine has been agreed upon in the loan contract. Then there is indemnification for the loss caused to the creditor through the delay of the borrower in repayment; finally, indemnification in case of risk of losing the principal.[2]

[1] *Sententiae*, IV, distinctio 15, questio 2, 22 *et seq.*

[2] *Sententiae*, IV, distinctio 15, questio 2, 17–19. See also C. R. S. Harris, *Duns Scotus*, Oxford, 1927.

V

THE LEGACY OF THE SCHOOLMEN

1. *Preparing the Way for Modern Times*

The Christian Church at the height of its spiritual domination over emperors, kings, lords, and villains, that is, from the eleventh to the fourteenth centuries, had to assert itself against two movements. First, in order to enforce its tenets on various heretic sects (Cathari, Waldenses, etc.), which looked back to primitive Christianity as their ideal of life and denied the lawfulness of private property and commerce; secondly, in order to make its ethics prevail in the transactions of trade and commerce, which were growing up on the basis of absolute property and self-interest in the revived towns of Western and Central Europe. In the towns, civil law, mostly of Roman origin, ruled between buyer and seller which, as Thomas Aquinas puts it, "secundum eas licitum est emptori et vendatori ut se invicem decipiant."[1] Contrary to the tolerance shown by the Roman lawyers to deceit in trading, the Church, in the spirit of Jewish and Patristic ethics, held that trade led easily to sin. In the words of Ecclesiasticus (27, 2), "As a nail sticketh between the joinings of the stones, so doth sin stick also between buying and selling."

The conflict between Roman law, Christian ethics, and

[1] Thomas Aquinas, *Summa*, Secunda Secundae, questio 77, articulus 1.

social heresies had been acute as far back as the first centuries of the Church. It had died down later, partly, perhaps, owing to the rise of the monasteries, which absorbed many of the communally-minded elements, and partly to the decay of the towns and decline of trading, which followed the disintegration of the Roman Empire. From the eleventh century onwards, however, the old problems—on the one hand, social-religious heresy, on the other, trade and commerce—rose up in renewed strength and demanded solution. The schoolmen in the various parts of Christendom set to work to incorporate private property into jus naturale, and to adapt, by compromise, Christian anti-individualist ethics to town life. We have seen the most prominent English schoolmen at work.

Private property, so the schoolmen argued, was established jure naturali et divino as the most beneficent arrangement for social life in the fallen state of man. Post lapsum the original and natural community of possessions was revoked, and the goods divided either by legitimate governmental power or by consent of the governed, which, though instituted by man-made law, partook of the essence of jus naturale. Alexander of Hales, Ricardus de Media Villa, Duns Scotus, and William of Ockham concur in this view.

Trade and commerce was declared lawful by Alexander of Hales, who regarded the transport of goods by the trader as labour worthy of a reward; furthermore, the trader or chapman, by conserving the goods against deterioration, arson, or larceny, deserves to be rewarded by society, which needs them. Ricardus de Media Villa demonstrated by economic reasoning that the trader's gain was not by any means owing to deceit, but to the service he rendered in equalizing supplies in the various regions of the earth. Duns Scotus thought trade highly useful to ordered social life, so that the gain of the trade was in the nature of a social salary.

In the strongest fortress of all, the prohibition of usury, many breaches were made by the English schoolmen. Wherever loss or risk was caused to the lender, he was entitled to damages from the borrower.

In the reasonings of the schoolmen, two considerations stand out most prominently as guiding stars. Whenever dialectic failed to remove doubt and misgiving, the schoolmen judged institutions from the point of their effect on the well-being and ordered life of society, as well as on the subordination of self-interest to the commonweal. These considerations guided and justified them in their endeavour for some sort of compromise between primitive Christian ethics and the changed circumstances in which modern life developed.

2. *William of Ockham*

We have so far dealt with Alexander of Hales, Ricardus de Media Villa, and Duns Scotus, omitting to deal with William of Ockham, for in economic matters he was a follower and not a leader. But, while adding nothing to the economic reasonings of his predecessors, he was in other respects the most revolutionary and influential of all scholastic pioneers of modern life. Ockham was one of those pioneers who prepared the way for the advance of

Western civilization from mediaeval to modern times. His activities far transcended those of the universities and colleges. He made history. His astonishingly keen, vehement, and unflinching contest with papal power, his ardent opposition to turning the Church into a vast system of economic and financial administration, made him the foremost pioneer of the Reformation. His renewal and strengthening of Nominalism, or the doctrine that the particular entities are the only palpable and positive realities, while universals are mere abstractions or names, without existence *extra animam*, was one of his most destructive weapons. Stripped of its philosophical terminology, Nominalism meant the negation of the universality of the Roman Church and the recognition of the national sovereignties and of individual consciences. And, by limiting, circumscribing, and confining the functions of reason to physical phenomena, he destroyed scholasticism itself, whose mission it was supposed to be to make faith intelligible. Reason could neither prove nor disprove metaphysical truths. It was idle to impose upon reason the task of demonstrating the existence of God and the validity of other theological tenets; it was altogether beyond the capacity of reason to enter the region of metaphysics. This region was governed by faith, the basis and mainstay of Christianity and ethics.

Ockham had one successor in England and two in Germany, viz. John Wycliffe, Martin Luther, and Immanuel Kant. Wycliffe's opposition to papal supremacy and Church property was in the tradition of Ockham, but there can be no doubt whatever that the latter, unshakable in his faith, would have condemned Wycliffe's theology as heretic. Martin Luther, in the first stage of his career, often appealed to the teachings of Ockham. Kant, in his *Critique of Pure Reason*, sets limits to the competence of reason; his emphasis on the inability of reason to reach the "Ding an sich"; his antinomies which by logical syllogisms prove and disprove the existence of God, the soul, and immortality, are one and all in the Ockhamite spirit, for they demonstrate the ineptness of logic and dialectic as instruments in the domain of metaphysics. Furthermore, Kant's *Critique of Practical Reason* (that is, ethics) is based on faith. The Germans called Kant *All-Zermalmer* (all destroyer), but he owed much to the Englishman William of Ockham.

3. *Influence on Modern Views*

Some mediaeval ideas which Ricardus used are found in economic and political writings of the sixteenth and seventeenth centuries, though there is no direct evidence that the writers knew their source. The schoolmen, however, were in those times still read by Englishmen. New editions of the schoolmen's folios were published, and scholastic ideas circulated in the universities and colleges. Two of those ideas deserve our attention by reason of their affiliation and development:

(i) From a dictum of Ricardus that the produce of labour belonged rightly to the labourer, and not to the lender of money which the labourer employed as his instrument ("homo dominus est sui laboris et industriae"), John Locke, who read the schoolmen, and the Labour socialists, who read Locke, drew two diametrically opposed conclusions. Locke used it as an argument in favour of private property;[1] while the socialists used it as an argument against capital. They argued that, since labour was the real producer of value, and since capital (money) was barren metal and did not breed money, the produce of labour ought to belong to the labourer. Hence, everything taken away from labour by capital was robbery.

(ii) The mediaeval idea adduced by Ricardus that the diversity of the natural endowments of the various countries rendered international trade a necessity and formed a common bond between men, is often to be met with in mercantilist writings.

"Surelie," declares John Hales, "common reason would that one region should healpe another when it lacketh. And therefore God hath ordained that no countrie should have all commodities, but that what one lacketh, another bringeth forth . . . to the entent that one maie know they have nede of anothers healpe and thereby Love and societie to grow amongst them all the more."[2] This was written about 1549. Half a century later (1601), Gerard Malynes writes that "God caused Nature to distribute her benefits, or his blessings to severall climates . . . to the ende that enterchangeably one commonweale should live with another."[3] Edward Misselden, in everything else the bitter opponent of Malynes, concurs in this that "it hath pleased God to invite as it were, one country to traffique with another, by the variety of things which the one hath and the other hath not, so that which is wanting to the one

[1] John Locke, *Of Government*, II, §§ 27, 40–42.

[2] John Hales, *A Discourse of the Common Weal*, ed. Lamont, p. 61. (This book will hereinafter be referred to as John Hales, *A Discourse*.)

[3] Gerard Malynes, *The Canker of England*, p. 6.

might be supplied by the other, that all might have sufficient."[1] Finally, Charles Davenant, writing at the end of the seventeenth century, sees in "the various products of different soils and countries an indication that Providence intended they should be helpful to each other, and mutually supply the necessities of one another."[2]

In the sixteenth and seventeenth centuries, when explorers went on their voyages of discovery, or when merchants were negotiating commercial treaties, the geographical argument about the diversity of climates and produce was put to much use. In 1553, Sir Hugh Willoughby and Richard Chancellor, on leaving for the north-eastern regions (White Sea, Archangel), were given a polyglot document addressed by Edward VI to all kings and princes, asking them to show friendliness to the bearers thereof, "for the God of Heaven and Earth, greatly providing for mankind, would not that all things should be found in one region, to the end that one should need of another; that by this means friendship and amitie might be established among all men . . . and farre countries." Merchants, by exchanging their wares, deserved, therefore, the furtherance and protection of the authorities. Sir Hugh Willoughby lost his life on that voyage, but Chancellor reached Moscow and received a charter from Ivan the Cruel, the Czar of Russia, in which it is said: "Forasmuch as God has planted all realmes and dominions in the whole world with sundry commodities, so as the one hath nede of the amity and commodities of

[1] Edward Misselden, *Free Trade*, 1622, p. 25.

[2] Charles Davenant, *Works*, vol. i, pp. 104–105. For a literary exposition of the geographic distribution of products see *Spectator*, No. 69, May 10, 1711, written by Addison.

the other, and by means thereof traffike is used from one to another, and amity thereby increased." The preamble goes on to recite all the blessings that commercial intercourse brings to mankind.

The actual reality of commercial intercourse during those centuries, however, was in direct contradiction with the ethical sentiment, bequeathed by mediaevalism, of mutual assistance and equal exchanges between the various regions of the earth. Universal Christendom was split into national economic units, endeavouring to get the better of one another. Their commercial activities were dictated by individual interests or by policies which were later known as the balance of trade. Francis Bacon, the most representative man of the period, formulated its fundamental principle when he declared that a country could only increase its wealth by exploiting other countries. "The increase of any estate must be upon the foreigner, for whatsoever is somewhere gotten is somewhere lost."[1]

[1] Francis Bacon, *Essays*, xv.

VI

THE AGE OF MERCANTILISM

GENERAL VIEW

1. *Definition*

English mercantilism may be defined as a set of policies and doctrines, successively designed:

(i) To use foreign trade as a means of bringing treasure (coin and bullion) into the King's exchequer or into the merchant's stock, and making it stay in the realm;

(ii) To protect the nascent manufactures by import duties;

(iii) To turn protective or prohibitive tariffs into instruments of defence and offence against economic and political rivals.

Mercantilist trading is thus easily differentiated from free trade, the ideal purpose of which is to promote reciprocal exchange of all sorts of commodities and commercial services among all nations, in order to enable them to produce or procure in the most profitable way the goods they need for the satisfaction of their mutual wants.

Till the last quarter of the seventeenth century all mercantilist reasoning may be expressed in the following syllogism:

(i) Money or treasure (coin and bullion) constitutes riches (wealth);

(ii) Foreign trade is the only means to bring money.

Hence, only foreign trade can bring riches, while home trade is but a mere transfer of goods from hand to hand, without enriching the realm.

This view is thus clearly distinguished from that of the succeeding manufacturing or industrial age, which regards the production of commodities as the main source of wealth.

Mercantilism rightly deserves its name, for it was the merchant (mercator) through whose operations the successive aim of the king and the trading community was to be effected. He was the dynamic agent of the outgoing mediaeval and incoming modern age. Mercantile capital played then the same part as industrial capital has played since the middle of the eighteenth century.

In England, mercantilism achieved its classic form. It guided the policy of personal monarchy, starting with the later Angevins, and it was followed up by the rising and triumphant mercantile class. It thus covered two political periods of English history—(i) from Edward I, or more systematically from Edward III, to Queen Elizabeth; and (ii) from the Stuarts to the accession of the Hanoverians. The basic idea remained throughout both periods the same—namely, getting treasure into the realm, but the methods employed for accomplishing that aim and end were different. In the first period, personal monarchy enacted so-called bullionist ordinances and statutes for that purpose. In the second period, the merchants attempted to accomplish that aim by the balance of trade policy. In passing from the first to the second period, that is, from personal monarchy to the merchant classes, mercantilism gradually changed from a system of bullionist and fiscal regulations into a policy and doctrine of international trade, foreign exchanges, and protection of the manufacturing and landed interests. From the last years of the seventeenth century onwards, some of the most important doctrinal elements of mercantilism were increasingly challenged. The only element that still preserved and even increased its vitality was protection by tariffs, and the use of foreign trade as one of the instruments of foreign politics.

The division of the age of mercantilism into two periods, with two different applications of its principle, as suggested here and will be made clear in the following pages, is, I believe, capable of rendering real service to the study and comprehension of English economic and social history from the thirteenth to the eighteenth century.

The doctrine, whose rough outlines we have drawn, will no doubt strike the modern mind as crude or, perhaps, as utterly irrational. Yet it was maintained for centuries, and it was promoted and defended partly by great legislators, partly by very shrewd and successful London merchants, as well as by intellectual workers, such as Francis Bacon, William Petty, and John Locke. The mercantilist doctrine, then, must have answered the interests and logic of its age. It will be our business to discover step by step how the doctrine grew quite naturally, that is, with necessity, out of the commercial, political, and ethical conditions of the realm.

2. *Importance of Coin and Bullion*

In the first period, the economic policy of the monarchs, that is, the later Angevins, Lancastrians, Yorkists, and Tudors, had for its political object the replenishing the exchequer with money (coin and bullion) as a means of making royal power supreme and enabling it to face any challenge of the barons and ecclesiastics or foreign princes. Money was indispensable to render it possible for the Crown to displace the centrifugal, rebellious baronial and ecclesiastical administrative bodies by creating of non-feudal elements a centralized royal administration and defence force in order to consolidate the Kingdom and secure the royal possessions outside the Kingdom. Without money the Crown could neither establish law and order at home nor make war on the Welsh, Scots, and the French. Moreover, the transition from the feudal structure of society to early modern life in town and village depended largely on money. It was the commutation of military and predial services into money payments that smoothed the path to the new social relations. And since Nature failed to endow England with gold and silver mines, the kings and later on the merchants used the staple commodities of the land to attract treasure from foreign countries.

Corresponding to the exalted position of kingship and the urge of the transition period was the social standing of money. The king set his effigy on it. He gave it valuation, which was thought to be its "spirit that giveth life,"[1] and thus transformed bullion into coin. The disposal of coin and bullion, or precious metals in general, and their

[1] W. A. Shaw, *History of Currency*, 1896, p. 5.

exchange were royal prerogatives. "The right of prerogative of exchange of bullion hath alwaie beene a flower of the Crowne . . . as from the utmost extancie of Record." It was King Henry I who appointed a Monetarius Regis "conjoyning in one person the office of Exchanger."[1] The king, by virtue of his prerogatives, could, arbitrarily, raise and reduce the valuation of the coin,[2] and—in case of State necessity—seize all the coin and bullion of his subjects. It was by virtue of this tradition that Charles I seized in 1640 the bullion which the merchants kept at the Tower.

Finally, lord and vassal and villain needed money for their freedom. And with money the Christian could buy himself free from purgatory. Money was treasure.

The need for treasure which dictated the trade policy of the English Crown ever since the end of the thirteenth century became an increasingly irresistible urge in the following two centuries, and finally controlled the trade policy of the mercantile classes. The revival and growth of trade and commerce in the West since the eleventh century was fed by German and Italian silver and gold. The Germans obtained precious metals from their mines

[1] *Cambium Regis*, 1628, written in defence of the proclamation of Charles I concerning the restoration of the office of the royal exchanger. It gives an outline of the history of that institution. See also Gerard Malynes, *Lex Mercatoria*, 1622, p. 380.

[2] The reader will be interested to learn that even as late as 1750 an English writer could declare, "The prince gives to every coin the ideal value . . . the arbitrary value which Sovereigns affix to the real money" (gold and silver). This was written by Malachy Postlethwayt, in his *Universal Dictionary of Trade and Commerce* (article, "Exchange"). The Dictionary went through six editions in the years 1750–1774, but it was based on the French dictionary of Savary, who wrote it in the reign of Louis XIV—a fact which explains a good deal.

in Saxony, Bohemia, the Tyrol, and Carinthia; the Italians obtained gold and silver from their lucrative traffic with the Byzantine Empire and North Africa. These facts explain why the Angevins favoured the Venetians, Genoese, Florentines, the German Easterlings, and the Steelyard, for these were the men who could bring precious metals to England.[1] As long as the growth of trade and commerce was gradual, the German and Italian supply of precious metals was fairly adequate. By the middle of the fifteenth century, however, the growth of trade was beginning to outstrip the available gold and silver stock and was increasingly pressing for a corresponding monetary expansion. English trade participated in that growth, as is evident from the fact that the same date—the middle of the fifteenth century—marked the beginning of the conversion of arable land into pasturage and the making of enclosures: English wool was in stronger demand than before. The need for larger metallic supplies became pressing and a veritable *auri sacra fames* seized the mercantile classes and the monarchs and drove them to search for new sources of supply or for easier access to the old sources, for ever since the conquest of Constantinople by the Turks the Levant traffic became onerous and uncertain, owing to Turkish exactions.

It may be noted *en passant* that those centuries formed the flourishing age of alchemy. Monarchs fitted out

[1] Like a good many other people, I was for a long time in doubt as to the linguistic origin of Sterling. Was it from Easterling or Starling? But after having read in the Rotuli Parl. (II, p. 172, § 61) the term *denier d'Esterling* all doubts were set at rest. I felt at once that in Norman French the silver penny was spoken of as "denier de Sterling."

laboratories for alchemists, who were supposed to possess the secret recipe for producing gold.

Money, it was felt, was not only the sinews of war and State, but of trade and commerce; it was the indispensable agency that stirred, quickened, and moved merchandise, the *vena porta*, the chief vein of the body politic—as Bacon characterized it. Money was called the "life-blood" that nourished and moved the whole body politic. Hobbes thought that money was the "sanguification of the commonwealth . . . and circulating nourisheth by the way every member of the body."[1]

In short, at the emergence of kingship and the various orders of Englishmen from the framework of feudalism, and at the subsequent rise of the mercantile class to national importance and consciousness, money appeared as the universal embodiment of wealth and superior to all material resources.

3. *The Mechanism of Bullionist Policy*

The kings sought to preserve and obtain treasure by the following legislative enactments and institutions: (i) numerous ordinances concerning bullion, laying an embargo on the exportation of coin, bullion, or plate; (ii) customs regulations, which levied heavy customs and subsidies on the export and import of commodities; (iii) for the better supervision of the customs, as well as

Francis Bacon, *Essays*, XII, XIX; Thomas Hobbes, *Leviathan*, ch. 24; Samuel Lamb, *Several Observations* (1659) in Somers Tracts, vol. vi, p. 468; Sam Fortrey, *England's Interest* (1663), ed. Hollander, p. 43.

quality of the staple commodities, certain English, Welsh, and Irish coast towns, and from about the middle of the fourteenth century the town of Calais, were made into staple towns, that is, the only places whereto the English staple commodities could be sent, weighed, and customed for export; the customs receipts, as well as a part of the purchase money for the sale of wool, if in foreign coin or bullion, were to go to the Mint for coinage or recoinage; (iv) the duty of the royal exchanger to execute the business of conveying bullion into the Mint and converting foreign coin into English rates and minting them into current coin; the exchanger was the delegate of the Crown in all money matters and wielded wide powers; (v) the instrument to make the bullion ordinances work were the regulations, the most famous of which were those of 14 Richard II, 18 Henry VI, 17 Edward IV, and 3 Henry VII, known as Statutes of Employment, which put the foreign importer under strict supervision (hosting) and made it incumbent upon him to employ the proceeds of his sales in the purchase and export of English commodities, since it was illegal to carry treasure out of the country, except for journey expenses.

The first reference to an ordinance of bullion is extant only in a missive of Edward I, written on March 9, 1303, to the Mayor of Southampton, on behalf of a merchant of Bayonne, whose money the searchers confiscated, "believing that he wished to carry the same to parts beyond the sea against our prohibition that no man should carry any money or silver in bullion out of our realm." It is not known in which year that ordinance was put into force, nor whether it was the first of its line. In 9 Edward

III a long ordinance concerning money was published, in which the following provision occurs:

"First, it is provided that no man of religion or other henceforth carry the sterling out of the realm of England, nor silver in plate, nor vessels of gold or silver, on pain of forfeiture of the money, plate or vessels that he shall carry, without special licence from us."[1]

Such ordinances or confirmations thereof were from time to time issued or again brought to the notice of the public by the kings and their officers. The last ordinance of bullion was issued by James I, June 11, 1622.[2]

Assuming that business practice and foreign exchanges conformed to the intentions of the royal enactments, the net result of such transactions was as follows:

When the foreign importer brought goods to England, he received the price in coin or bullion, but he could not get away with the money and had to spend it on English goods for export, on outward customs, and on his travelling expenses. So that the whole transaction was reduced to barter between the English and foreign traders, that is, commodity for commodity, while the coin always remained in the king's dominion. Considering that English staple commodities could always find ready vent it was thought that the bullion ordinances, the employment statutes, customs, subsidies, and impositions, would bring plenty of treasure into the country and keep it there.

The mercantile enactments of the Angevin kings could have no regard to the nationality of the trade or the pro-

[1] Reprinted in Bland, Brown, Tawney, *Select Documents*, pp. 216–218.

[2] Proclamatio contra exportationem bullionis. Rymer-Sanderson, *Foedera*, vol. xvii, folio 376.

venance of his commodities, for, as it will be shown, the national idea is of later origin. Monarchy was in its mercantile and financial policy quite universalist. It was for so-called freedom of trade, which, in fact, handed over most of the export trade to the merchant-stranger. Magna Charta, section 41, the Carta Mercatoria of Edward I, and many ordinances of Edward III, Richard II, etc., favoured the foreign trader, for he brought treasure either as loans to the Crown or paid in gold and silver inward and outward customs to the Exchequer. The English trader had to struggle hard in order to obtain a part of the foreign trade. He had even to fight for the appointment of Englishmen as customs officials; the kings preferred foreign "customers and searchers." In 27 Edward III, an ordinance was enacted handing over the whole export of staple commodities to foreigners to the total exclusion of the English. Though it was repealed in 34 Edward III, it was characteristic enough of the pro-alien attitude of the king. It was only with the Yorkists that some national sentiment began to make headway in economic legislation. As far as national gains in political and economic respects were hereby achieved they but constituted the indirect or fortuitous results of the assertion and predominance and needs of royal power and had nothing to do with English national sentiment, of which the Angevins could not have been conscious.

4. *The Ethics of the Angevin Trade Legislation*

To the modern mind all those ordinances and statutes might appear to have been vexatious, mischievous, tyrannical, or extortionate. And they so appeared to an acute economist, Professor Richard Jones, who analysed them in a much quoted paper, entitled "Primitive Political Economy" (*Edinburgh Review*, April 1847). He ascribed them to the "darkness of the age." Those enactments, when isolated from the social and moral background of their time, are undoubtedly baffling to the modern mind, but it would be quite unhistorical to condemn them off-hand. We are apt to forget that the mediaeval regulations, ordinances, and statutes had their ultimate authority in Christian precepts, or were, to say the least, brought into some relation to the conceptions of what the Christian man was taught to regard as godly or sinful in his daily life. We have seen how schoolmen and canonists were wrestling with the problems of ethics and economics in order to bring them into a certain harmony. Mediaeval legislators, no less than modern legislators, were actuated by causes and reasons, by principles and their corollaries, suggested to them by the economic and political circumstances and the ethical attitude of their time.

The economic and political causes were given above in some detail. The kings were in need of bullion, and foreign trade was the most efficient means to bring it into the realm. The merchant-stranger could supply it, and the native merchant was still unable to displace him. And as in late mediaeval and early modern times the national idea was not yet developed, while the principle of Christian universalism was still active, the foreign merchant had priority over the English one.

The ethical reasons were: in the fourteenth and fifteenth centuries, England was still, on the whole, a static society, though not without some ominous forebodings of coming change. She was bent on preserving her economy rather than enriching it by new methods. Only the king's treasure was to be made more plentiful, since his governance was regarded as the highest good. Parliament was aiming at stabilizing rather than changing the relations between the various orders of society. Canon Law was, in theory at least, still a good guide in man's economic activities, and it demanded commutative justice, that is, equality of exchanges, and no gain on money. The bullion ordinances and the statutes of employment embodied also those principles. They were to prevent making money an object of gain, and they turned the exchanges within the realm into barter—commodity for commodity; they prevented buying more than we sold, that is, they intended to prevent buying luxuries, costly apparel, wines; they thus conformed to the intentions of the Sumptuary Laws.

Indeed, the Sumptuary Laws, enacted and often renewed and extended in the centuries from the reign of Edward III to Elizabeth, may serve as a demonstration of the policy of King and Parliament to preserve the equilibrium of society and to keep its members within the bounds of their respective "estate and degree." Those laws had no doubt economic motives, that is, not to lessen the treasure of the realm by buying more than it sold, but their ultimate appeal was to ethical self-restraint in order not to incur "the great displeasure of God."[1]

Those ordinances, statutes, and laws were all enacted in a spirit eminently conservative. The prevailing tradi-

[1] Tawney and Power, *Tudor Economic Documents*, vol. i, p. 327. This collection of documents will hereafter be referred to as *T.E.D.*)

tional conceptions, moral, economic, and social, were to be safeguarded and defended from the gradual encroachments of the new money economy, which was dynamic in its nature.

They were however, in effect, increasingly directed against the new trading classes which were growing up with the growth of international trade. And their interests could not develop unless those laws were abrogated. The exemption of money from gainful employment, equal scales of purchases and sales, made all profitable commerce impossible. The English merchant could neither suffer the priority of the foreign merchants, who had the opportunity of enriching themselves at the expense of the realm, nor could he find satisfaction in Canon Law. He grew anti-universalist and anti-Canonist. He grew anti-mediaeval. And he began his march to victory in the reign of Henry VIII.

With regard to the political influence of the merchants it was said in 1559 "that since 1 Henry VIII there could never been won any good law or order which touched their liberty or estate, but they stayed it."[1] Good law or order meant, of course, in those times laws inspired by mediaeval conceptions.

By the middle of the sixteenth century, the career of Canon Law was at an end. A year after Thomas More's martyrdom Thomas Cromwell, the most advanced representative of the rising middle class, put a stop to the

[1] Lord Salisbury's MSS., Hist. MSS. Comm., I, 164, No. 14, quoted by W. Hooper, LL.D., in *English Historical Review*, vol. xxx, p. 433. This statement is of historical importance. It is the evidence of a contemporary that mercantile capital was a powerful social factor two decades prior to the Reformation.

teaching of Canon Law in the Universities. Trade developed, the number of merchants grew rapidly, and the new class formulated policies of English trade; that is, it concentrated its efforts on English economic and political matters. In essence, though not yet in name, the balance of trade became its guiding star. The scales of exports and imports should no more be kept level, but the exports should overbalance the imports.

This trade policy was increasingly promoted by the mercantile class through Parliament, and had for its result the ousting of the merchant-stranger, the fostering and protecting of native trade and manufacture, or, as sixteenth-century writers call it, "artificialte." Balance of trade—and from the beginning it meant a favourable balance[1]—setting people to work, fostering foreign trade and manufacture, became since about 1550 the guiding rules. The merchants were laying the foundation of economic nationalism. They withdrew from mediaeval universalism and concentrated their efforts on English economic and political life. They created the English national idea, English patriotism. True, this policy meant retreat and retrenchment, but in this restricted circle it made England the centre from which the national energies should radiate far and wide.

The gradual abandonment of mediaeval universalism in commerce and religion was preceded in philosophy by the abandonment of the Universals in favour of the Particulars (Nominalism). Lightning preceded the thunder.

[1] The addition of the adjective "favourable" to qualify the term "balance of trade" is of later origin, perhaps as late as the eighteenth century.

The individualization of society through the progress of money economy went on apace, though not without reactions to the past, which found expression in royal ordinances and measures calculated to check those developments or to restore the *status quo ante.*

5. *The two Periods of Mercantilism*

Divisions of history into periods, apart from those of mere chronology, are not clear-cut. They are drawn by historians, guided by theory. The divisions drawn in the former chapters are, therefore, still to be established, for there have been authoritative economic writers who thought to have found protectionist and balance of trade policies in Angevin enactments and, on the other hand, bullionist conceptions in later mercantilism. These objections have to be dealt with.

No doubt, in the first period, that is, the bullionist period and freedom of trade for the aliens, some ordinances were enacted which implied protection of native trade and fiscal discrimination against the alien. For, whenever kings were in need of grants and subsidies, and this was often enough the case, the Commons, wonderfully alert for an opportunity to promote English commerce and liberty, asserted themselves and obtained greater consideration for their interests. Those concessions were, however, either temporary or not effective.[1] The principle of freedom of trade as guaranteed by Magna Charta

[1] The anonymous author of "Policies to reduce Englande unto a prosperous wealthe and Estate" (1549) points out that in 3 and 22 Edward IV, 1 Richard III, and 1 Henry VII "requeste was made by dyvers artifficers that certain wares as poinctes, lace, gyrdelles, rybondes, purses and pouches, knyves, hangers and dyvers other kindes

(section 41), by the Carta Mercatoria, further by 9 Edward III, 18 Edward III, 25 Edward III, 2 Richard II, 5 Richard II, 11 Richard II, 16 Henry IV, etc., etc., which formed the charters of the alien merchants, that is, the Hansa, the Italians, and the Flemish, was, on the whole, observed to the end of the first period, though the native merchants often raised their voice, sometimes crescendo by rioting, against the favours shewn by the Crown to their foreign competitors. Even as late as 1558, Sir Thomas Gresham could direct the attention of Queen Elizabeth to the privileges of the Hansa (Steelyard) which put the native trader at a disadvantage. "Whereas," he writes, "your own merchants payeth outwards fourteen pence upon a cloth custom, they pay but nine pence; and likewise, for all such wares as was brought into the realm, your own ware merchants payeth twelve pence upon the pound, the Steelyard paid but three pence upon the pound."[1]

We find, further, as we learn from Adam Smith, that even in the second period of mercantilism the bullionist notions were prevalent.[2] Smith is quite right in his observation. There were in the years between 1650 and 1750 mercantilists who identified money with wealth, but this anachronism vanishes as soon as we penetrate the essence of the balance of trade doctrine. This matter is cleared up in a later chapter.[3]

shoulde be utterly prohibited upon payne of forfayture to be brought into the realme, and dyverse stattutes was then made, but . . . those stattutes toke litell effect" (*T.E.D.*, iii, p. 332).

[1] Burgon's *Life and Times of Sir Thomas Gresham*, vol. i, p. 483.

[2] Adam Smith, *Wealth of Nations*, book 4, ch. 1.

[3] See *infra*, section ix.

Another economic writer, the above-mentioned Misselden, in his zeal to defend the principle of the balance of trade against bullionist policy, projects it into the past in order to shew that it was no novelty and thus justify it in the proper English way, which is governed by precedent. "This balance of trade is no conceit or novelty, but has been the wisdom and policy even of elder times," and he reproduces "an ancient balance of trade which is said to be found upon Record in the Exchequer in the 28 year of Edward III." This balance of trade yielded a surplus of export over import to the amount of £255,214."[1] However, from a single instance no general inference can be drawn. It is further to be remembered that 28 Edward III was the height of that King's war on France, so that there must have been a large export of wool for war expenditure and not for normal trade.

Finally, Professor William Cunningham advances the opinion that in the reign of Richard II a high official of the Mint, Richard Aylesbury, "appears to have anticipated the doctrine of the balance of trade" but "Parliament adopted a bullionist experiment, while Richard Aylesbury appears to have been a mercantilist—to adopt terms which were in vogue in the seventeenth century."[2] I do not know what text Professor Cunningham was working upon, at any rate the original text as given in *Rotuli Parl.* III, pp. 126–127, cannot by any effort of imagination be construed into a balance of trade doctrine. Aylesbury did no more than recommend the execution of

[1] Edward Misselden, *Circle of Trade*, 1623, pp. 116–118.

[2] Cunningham, *Growth of English Industry, Early and Middle Ages*, ed. 1922, pp. 395–396.

the bullionist policy, as given in former chapters. The facts are these. In 1381–1382 the officers of the Mint informed the King that there was a deficiency of money and that the coin which was in circulation was getting deteriorated. They warned the King that "If you do not apply a speedy remedy thereto in short time to come, where you think to have five shillings you will not have four shillings." The five officers were: Richard Leye, Lincoln (goldsmith), Crantern, John Hoo, Richard Aylesbury. Several questions as to the cause of the money crisis and the remedies to be applied were addressed to them, but we can refer to the main question only, viz. foreign trade. The text is in Norman French, but we translate some parts of it into English.

Leye declared: "First, as to this that no gold or silver comes into England, but that which is in is carried beyond the sea, I maintain that it is because the land spends too much in (foreign) merchandise, as in grocery, mercery and furs, or wines, red, white and sweet, and also in exchanges made to the Court of Rome in divers ways. Wherefore the remedy seems to me to be that each merchant bringing merchandise into England takes out of the commodities of the land as much as his merchandise aforesaid shall amount to; and none carry gold or silver beyond the sea, as it is ordained by Statute. . . . And so me seems that the money that is in England will remain, and great quantity of money and bullion will come from beyond the sea. . . ."

Lincoln said that instead of money the Church should send merchandise to the Court of Rome. Crantern and Hoo concurred in the view of Leye that the main remedy consisted in seeing to it that the imports should not exceed the exports. The last to reply was Richard Aylesbury, whose opinion we reproduce in his Norman French:

"Si la marchandie qui va hors d'Engl' soit ben & justement gouverne la monnaie qui est en Engl' demeurra, & grant pleinte de monoie vendra de part dela. C'est assavoir que plus de merchandise ne veigne deinz la Roialme que la value n'est del marchandise denizeins qu'est issent par dehors la Roialme."

The text is as clear as it could be made. Aylesbury spoke fully in the sense of the mercantile policy of the first period: The exports should be equal to the imports, that is, not to buy more than one sells: merchandise for merchandise; execution of the Statutes. By these means the exports would always cover the imports, and money would not leave the country, but would increase through customs and subsidies and would remain within the realm. There is in the text no trace whatever of the balance of trade.

The confusion about the essential characteristics of two periods of mercantile policy appears to be widespread —Professor Cunningham made Aylesbury an international celebrity—and it can only be dissipated by marking them off from one another: The first period was for the principle of commutative justice, that is, equality of exchanges; this was the ethical basis of the bullion ordinances and Statutes of Employment. The second period developed the doctrine of the overbalancing exports, which became known as balance of trade.

The term "balance of trade," as it was employed ever

since it arose in the first quarter of the seventeenth century and referred to by such writers as Edward Misselden, Francis Bacon, Thomas Mun, John Locke, Isaac Newton, as well as Adam Smith (when the latter is opposing mercantilism), always implied inequality of trading accounts. It immediately suggested that a differential sum, a balance, was due to either of the business parties. It meant either a favourable or unfavourable balance of trade as the result of business transactions.

Professor Cunningham and his followers—and there are many in Britain and abroad—never realized that the formula "balance of trade" was one of the first economic expressions of the merchant and trading classes in opposition to the mediaeval principle of equality of exchanges, for they assumed that equal exchanges brought no advantage. Owing to that misunderstanding Professor Cunningham and his followers made mediaevalist statesmen stress the principle of the balance of trade. Now, this is exactly what they did not do, for they still adhered to mediaeval ethics and enjoined the various orders of the realm to forgo luxuries and costly apparel, so that imports should not exceed exports.

To suggest, as Professor Cunningham (who was also a doctor of divinity) does suggest, that in the fourteenth century, that is, at the height of mediaevalism, a high officer of the King's Mint could advise His Majesty to adopt the balance of trade policy, is no less an anachronism than to suggest, for instance, that Cardinal Wolsey might have advised Henry VIII not to debase the coinage, but to "go off gold and silver," that is, to close the Mint and leave all the bullion in storage at the Tower, and to print and issue instead paper notes for groats, testons, and nobles.

Researches at the Record Office, the Manuscript Department of the British Museum, and knowledge of the Statutes of the Realm do not make a historian yet. He must also possess the gift of entering into the spirit of the past with which he deals, and thinking the thoughts of the leading agents of the period.

The period in which Aylesbury lived was the century of Duns Scotus, Ockham, Wycliffe, and Canon lawyers, who only permitted gain in trade as a wage or salary. It precluded all thought of connecting trade with a policy of gain upon the foreigner. When Aylesbury was thinking of the depletion of treasure he meant the King's treasure, which must be replenished by the then prevailing legislative measures, and by self-restraint, that is, by not buying more than the country sells, but never by consistently selling more to the foreigner than he buys from the country. The latter idea was born at least a hundred and fifty years after the advice of the five Mint officials had been given to Richard II, and then it took seventy years more to find for the new-born idea the term "balance of trade." A new society had first to emerge from mediaevalism, and a new economy, with ideas adequate to it, had to be brought into being before a new trade policy could be formulated.

I have done now with polemical criticism. The general view, in giving the broad outlines of English mercantilism, will, I believe, serve as a reliable guide in the following detailed treatment of the subject. All the questions touched upon in the general view will be treated from a purely economic point of view, as they arose in the sixteenth and seventeenth centuries and which resulted in the formulation of theories about exchanges, the essence of money and value, and international trade.

VII

SIXTEENTH CENTURY ECONOMICS

1. *Price Revolution and Money Difficulties*

The sixteenth century is the *saeculum mirabile* in modern English history. It was the age of adolescence of the middle class. A great unrest, a vehement dynamic drive, was working the English mind, and it grew progressively in intensity and potency as the century advanced. Merchants and seamen, brimful with vitality and adventurous spirit, bent on voyages for material values, theologians, statesmen, poets, and dramatists, spurred by an infinite desire to discover new religious, social, and psychological values, and all driven by mighty economic and moral forces, were laying the foundations of modern England and the British Empire. It was an age resounding with the clash between the old and the new—a dramatic age.

It is a great temptation to an historically-minded writer to leave his special, limited field of research for the larger aspects of the period of adolescence of the English middle class which is generally known as the Tudor period. One is tempted to comprehend all its aspects as a whole—from Thomas More and John Hales to Francis Bacon, from Cardinal Wolsey, Thomas Cromwell and Thomas Gresham to Lord Burghley, from Marlowe and Jonson to Shakespeare, from Hawkins, Drake, and Frobisher to Raleigh, but there is still more spadework to be done in order to obtain a full view of the foundations of the *saeculum mirabile*.

Our immediate business is mercantilism, that is, to show how the search for treasure—the great passion that mobilized the Italians, Portuguese, Spaniards, French, and English to embark on uncharted seas and discover new lands—led to inquiries about the essence of money, to the formulation of the balance of trade doctrine, and to the promotion of manufacture as the most advantageous means of getting treasure through a plus of exports.

Apart from the agricultural changes brought about by the conversion of arable land into sheep runs—itself the effect of commercial development—there were two economic causes which may be regarded as having been at the bottom of the general unrest—namely, the rise of prices and the scarcity of money. The rise of prices was going on throughout the whole of the century, while the complaint about the scarcity of money, though intermittent, was more acute in the second half of the century, despite the influx of treasure from the West Indies and from the trade with Spain, France, and Flanders, which was in those years more abundant than ever before. Contemporary evidence on this point is unmistakable. "The plentie of treasure," writes the anonymous editor of Hales's *Discourse* in 1581, is "far more in these our dayes than ever our forefathers have sene in times past. Who doth not understand of the infinite sums of gold and silver, which are gathered from the Indies and other countries and yearly transported unto these costes."[1] And William Harrison, in his *Description of England* of his days

[1] John Hales, *A Discourse*, p. 187.

(1577–87), paints a dazzling picture of the new country houses, merchants' habitations, replete with costly tapestries, furniture, and plate.[1] Yet, the complaint about scarcity of money and the dearth (rise of prices) was general and formed the main stimuli to economic inquiries into the nature of money, price fluctuation, and the effect of plentifulness and scarcity of money on prices. These speculations, though not exhaustive, went a long way towards a solution of the riddle of money.

2. *The "Dearth" and Debasement of the Coinage*

The rise of prices, or the dearth, as it was called, grew progressively, and reached by the middle of the sixteenth century considerable proportions, which affected all estates and orders of the realm. The rise of prices was not uniform. Some commodities were "dearer by the thirde parte, yea almost the one half dearer than before time," while the price of other commodities, particularly those that were imported, rose by two or three hundred per cent. It was a perplexing question, all the more as there was no scarcity of victuals nor of any other commodities. "There was never more plentie of cattell than there is nowe," writes Hales, "and yet it is scarcitie of things which commonly maketh dearthe. This is a mervelous dearthe that in such plentie cometh, contrary to his kynd."

But though "every estate fyndith hymself greevede by this universall dearthe" it is the men "as have theire lyvinges and stypends rated at a certeyntie" that are suffering most, "such as common laborers at six pence the

[1] W. Harrison, *A Description of England*, ed. 1587, pp. 238–243.

daye, jorneymen of all occupations, servinge men at forty shillings the yeare, and gentlemen, whose landes are let oute by them . . . for terme of yeares, so as they can not enhance the rent thereof, and yet have the price enhanced to them of everiething they bie."

Searching for the cause of the dearth, many people were inclined to ascribe it to dishonest manipulations by the merchants, "for what oddes soever theare happen to be in exchange of things the merchants can espie it anone" and make the best of it and "save themselves in every alteration."[1] In verse and prose, in petitions to the Crown and its Chancellors, in sermons to the congregation, the merchants were charged with having caused the rise of prices by dishonest exchanges in exporting native commodities at low prices and importing foreign commodities at high prices, which then raised the price in the home market.[2]

As long as the cause of the dearth was ascribed to the moral turpitude of a certain group of human beings, no light could be thrown on the nature of money. It was merely playing battledore and shuttlecock with the question. "Some thought the husbandmen were guilty who charged high prices for victuals, whereupon the

[1] John Hales, *A Discourse*, pp. 30–37.

[2] As a sample of the criticism levelled at the merchants the following may serve. It was written about 1530 by a strongly patriotic writer, about whose antecedents nothing certain is known. "All merchauntes . . . are commonly pore men's sones naturale born to labour for their lyvinge, which after they be bounde prentises to be merchauntes, all their labour, study and policy is by bying and selling to gete singler richis from the commonaltie . . . and lyveth by other menes work, and of naught risith to great richis, entending nothing else but to gete richis which knoweth no common weale" (*T.E.D.*, vol. iii, pp. 126–129).

husbandmen said that the fault was with the noblemen who raised the rents and making enclosures. Noblemen said the fault was with the merchants and artificers for selling everything dearer than in past times which causes everyman to make the most of his owne. Finally some councillors declared that by reason of the base money coined in the latter end of King Henry VIII, all foreign commodities sold dearer, which made afterwards the commodities of the Realme also to rise."[1]

Those who saw the cause of the dearth in the debasement of the coinage took the first step towards the understanding of the nature of money. Their view was, for a time, largely accepted and became current by the middle of the century:

"O most nobell Kinge,

Consyder well this thinge!

This coyne by alteracion
Hath brought this desolacion
Which is not yet all knowen

What myschiff it hath sowen."[2]

3. *John Hales on the Nature of Money*

In 1581, a certain W.S., into the personality of which it is irrelevant to inquire, brought out a quarto volume

[1] Gerard Malynes, *Canker of England*, 1601, pp. 90–91; *Id. Lex Mercatoria*, 1622, pp. 63–65. Compare Hales, *A Discourse*, pp. 38–48, where the same ideas are elaborately dealt with.

[2] *T.E.D.*, voi. iii, p. 36.

under the title *A Briefe Conceipte of Inglish Policie*, which may be regarded as the beginning of British political economy. The treatise was reprinted in 1751, 1808, 1813, 1876 by various publishers, one of whom thought to have discovered under the letters W.S. the name of William Shakespeare. In 1893 it was edited under the title *A Discourse of the Commonweal of this Realm of England*, by Miss Elizabeth Lamond. The editing may serve as a model for such literary ventures, though not easily imitated or duplicated. She sent the book out with an introduction—the product of vast researches—proving with a certainty which is all but absolute that it was John Hales (a member of Parliament in 1548, a member of the Commission on Enclosures in 1549, a promoter of learning, a reformer imbued with warm sympathy for the dispossessed peasantry) who wrote it in 1549. Miss Lamond writes that "W.S. had little to do with the composition of the book; he erased a few phrases and made one important addition" about the influx of West Indian treasure contributing to the rise of prices in the second half of the sixteenth century.

Hales worked with great zeal against the injury done to English agriculture and the peasantry by the conversion of arable land into sheep runs and by violent and unjust enclosures, the effects of which were seen in ruined townships and the impoverishment of the commonalty. As long as Protector Somerset lived it was possible for Hales to go on working for his ideas, though the Earl of Warwick subjected him to the fate of all honest reformers, that is, of being charged with fomenting sedition among the labouring population, which was in the years 1548 and 1549 in a state of ferment. Hales wrote a defence, in which he says, "There was never any man yet that went aboute any good thynge eyther for the advancement of Goddes glory or for the common welthe of his country, but his reward was slander of a great many. This is the onlye way and means for such as passe more on the world than God, more on the pryvat profett, than on the commonwealth. Such is the corrupte nature of man, he passythe not what he saythe, nor what he dothe, so that he may satisfie his ungodly desires and fylthe pleasures. . . . What part played Demetrius, the sylver smythe, when Paul went about to brynge the Ephesians to Christes religion? Dyd not he forthwith assemble the compayne of his occupation and inculked into their heddes that Paul preached sedition? His mind was not on the honour of Diana which he so often repeted, but on his gayne," that was endangered by Paul's preaching.

Hales was an economic reformer on individualist lines. He regarded common possession of land and all other things as not practicable. Individual possession was most appropriate, since man was covetous and most allured by profit, and where the law interfered too much with profit "men would defraud the law." He even pleads for the liberty of the farmers to sell their corn "as freely as men maie doe their other thinges," so that agriculture should become profitable "and everie man naturally will follow that wherein he seeth most profit," but self-interest must be so guided as to serve also the common interests of the country. The desire for gain could not be eradicated; covetousness was one of the passions working in man's heart, like any other passion; but the opportunities for gain should be so fashioned by law as to make self-interest coincide with common interest (pp. 121–122).

Hales exhibits all the marks of transition from mediaeval to modern times. Mediaeval in sentiment, modern in practice. He combines ethical views with mercantilist aims. "We are not born to ourselves, but partly to our country . . . and partly to our friends and neighbours. The image of God is in man, whose propertie is ever to do good to others, to distribute his goodness to others abroad" (p. 14). We owe it to our own country to increase its wealth. Treasure is the sinews of State and war: "Wise men saie that in peace men must looke and provide for warre," since "the iniquitie of man is suche as they cannot be longe withowte warre." Therefore "a prince ought to have greate treasure or else his subiectes agaynst all events." The treasure is to be procured by industry and frugality: by working up our raw materials into valuable goods, and by eschewing foreign trifles and luxuries. By restricting imports and "yf we kepe within us much of owr commodities, we must spare manie other thinges that we have now from beyond the seas; for we must alwaies take hede that we bie no more of strangers than we sell them; (for so wee shoude empoverishe owrselves and enriche them.) For he weare no goode husband that will bie more in the market than he selleth there againe" (pp. 84, 113, 62–63). He is in principle for equality of exchanges, since avarice is the fundamental cause of all evil (p. 112), but he also expressed views which belong to the second period of mercantilism, that is, to the balance of trade doctrine. Hales thought it necessary to admonish his countrymen not to export native raw materials, but to work them up into goods, the value of which consisted mainly in craftsmanship, since such goods brought in new riches in gold and silver. Much of the new riches would be "clear gain" and would assist the country in obtaining reserves of precious metals for cases of emergency, as well as in recovering much of the treasure that, owing to our "grossness" and ineptitude, had been lost to the stranger (pp. 65, 87).

The *Discourse* is written, like the *Utopia* of Sir Thomas More, which evidently served him in composition as a model in the form of a dialogue between a doctor (probably of divinity or law), a knight, a merchant, a husbandman, and a craftsman, who gave their reasons "for the matter intended, as against it" . . . and are "rehersing the common and universall greifes that men complaine on now a dayes," and seeking for "the causes and occasions of the same" as well as for remedies to be pursued (Preface).

The central theme is the dearth and the impoverishment of the realm through an excess of imports, mostly of foreign trifles. The *dramatis personae* are searching for the causes thereof, and this leads them to a discussion on money, debasement of the coinage, as well as on the sources of treasure.

The husbandman is of opinion that enclosures are the real cause. The noblemen are now demanding such high rents that he is forced to enhance the price of victuals, and if those are dear everything must go up in price. The doctor and the knight do not admit that enclosures were the cause of the dearth; enclosures, says the doctor, if made in a legal way and with compensation for the tenants in common, far from diminishing the production of victuals, raise agriculture to a more productive level. He is even of opinion that the best means to improve agriculture would be to divide up the common lands into severalties, so that each former tenant in the common lands should own his portion and enclose it for himself. The real injury of sudden and violent enclosures, which put so many farmers out of their livings, is not economic, but political. They embitter the peasantry and make it disposed to tumults and rebellion: moreover, those enclosures and the conversion of arable land into sheep runs diminish the population, hence also the strength of the commonwealth (pp. 47–50).

After the husbandman has had his opportunity for impugning enclosures as the cause of the dearth, the merchant expresses the view that "we merchants paye dearer for everie thynge that cometh over the sea . . . because they of beyond the sea will not receive our monie for their wares, as they were glad in times past to doe." It was then the debasement of the coinage that caused the dearth—a view in which the knight could not concur, since money "is but a token to go from man to man. And sithe it is stricken with the Kinges seall to be currant, what maketh it the mattire what metall it be, yea though it be but leather or paper?" The knight represents those who believe that it is the prerogative of the King to give valuation to the coin and that money is but a number of counters to reckon by, a conventional thing of no intrinsic value, or simply a measure to indicate the price of commodities. It is the schoolmen's saying that "money is not by virtue of its substance, but of the law," which coincides with the belief of the adherents of personal monarchy that it is in the King's pleasure to make and unmake money, to raise and lower its valuation.

Those views and traditions offer the doctor the occasion to reveal the nature of money, and he rejoins:

"You saie but as most part of men do saie, and yet they be far from the trweth." Were a king or an emperor able to valuate coin as he might think fit there would never be any dearth or scarcity of money. Experience, however, shows that this is not the case, though a king would gladly remedy those inconveniences if he could. It may be admitted that "a man at the first blushe would thinke that a king in this realme might doe this easily, and make what coin he would to be currant, and of what estimation it pleased him. But he who so thinketh, marketh but the termes, and not the thinges that are understanded by some." The truth is that money is esteemed for its substance and the quantity of the substance and not for its denomination. Gold and silver have a value of their own on the score of their utility and rarity, and they are most suitable to serve as money by reason of other qualities. They are "wares in so small weight most in value, and least cumbersome to carie, and least subject to detriment . . . and may be cut and divided in most pieces and portions without anie losse, to be as the meane to exchange all other wares by." Moreover, "money is, as it weare, a storehouse of anie commoditie ye would have . . . and is most universally currente yf it be of gold and silver."

Therefore, "gold and silver are the stuffe most meete

for coin to be stricken in. . . . Then I told you rarietie recommendeth the said metalls of gold and silver yet more; for as they doe excell in qualities, so againe nature seemeth to have laid them up in a farther warde than her other gyftes, to show us that all far thinges are rare, and that the farest thinges, as they be hardest to be attained, so they be the most esteemed. Yf glasse, as Erasmus saith, weare as rare as silver, it should be as deare as silver" (pp. 69–75, 114).

The real cause of the dearth, thinks the doctor, can now be revealed. If a number of coins weighing one ounce of standard silver is the price of, say, ten yards of cloth, then the same number of coins weighing but half an ounce of standard silver would only buy five yards of cloth. And then people would say cloth got much dearer than before. In truth, the price of cloth has not changed, but the price of the coin has fallen, because it contains now much less standard silver than before, and we must give double the number of coins. And although the number of coins doubled they contain no more than one ounce of standard silver. "The alteracion of the coyne is the chiefest and principall cause of the universall dearth. . . . To conclude, I thinke this alteracion of the coyne to be the first originall cause that strangers first selles their wares dearer to us; and that maketh all farmers . . . agayne to sell their commodities dearer," and then everything gets dearer (104–105).

This, for its time, enlightened view of money was not uniformly adhered to. Hales sometimes relapsed, as if pulled back by tradition, into the schoolmen's conception of money as merely a measure and looked for support to "Aristotle, the sharpest philosopher of witt that ever was" (p. 109).

Hales's mercantilist views on treasure, manufacture and protection are cited in later chapters. John Hales died in 1571, the year in which Thomas Mun was born.

4. *Influx of West Indian Treasure*

The interpretation of the dearth as being due to the debasement of the coinage looked plausible enough and was widely, though not universally, accepted. The original Tower pound standard silver was $\frac{222}{240}$, that is, with alloy, it gave 240 pennies.[1] The debasement in the Angevin period had been inconsiderable; serious debasement began only in the fifteenth century. In 13 Henry IV the pound standard silver had to yield 360 pennies; in 49 Henry VI, 450 pennies, and it went on growing worse in the reign of Henry VIII, "that profuse and bloody King" as Ruding calls him, when "our coins were reduced to the lowest degree of fineness which ever disgraced the English Mint. Silver was four ounces fine and eight ounces alloy."[2] In 36 Henry VIII, the pound silver had to yield 576 pennies. Instead of the original 20.5 Troy grains, the penny contained 5.0 grains.[3] In 2 Elizabeth (1559–60) a reform

[1] It is interesting to note that at the time of writing these lines (1937) the pound silver gives likewise 240 pence, the ounce silver being priced at about 20 pence.

[2] Ruding, *Annals of the Coinage*, ed. 1840, i, p. 310.

[3] For the purpose of forming more objective views on the alteration of the coinage in those centuries the following passage, taken from Thomas Mun's *England's Treasure* (ch. viii), may be of use. "In all occasions of want or plenty of money in the Kingdom we do ever

of the coinage was carried through in England, while the coins struck for Ireland were still more debased and the ratio of fine to alloy was 3.9.

The reform and stabilization of the English coinage proved no remedy against the "dearth." The rise of prices, far from being checked, grew more and more pronounced. The debasement of the coinage in the reign of Elizabeth's predecessors could then not have been the efficient cause of the dearth. And another argument told strongly against debasement having caused the rise of prices. The dearth was not confined to England, but prevailed also in countries where no debasement had taken place. It was gradually recognized as a European phenomenon, as a universal price revolution.

What, then, was its cause?

The answer came in the third quarter of the sixteenth century, when the growing influx of American precious metals had spread from Spain, where the Conquistadors had brought it, to South Germany, France, the Low Countries, and at last, but not least, to England. It finally became manifest that money being a commodity, abundance lowered its price and scarcity raised its price, that is, in case of abundance of money more pieces of silver

find divers men, who using their wits for a remedy to supply the first and to preserve the last . . . say that the raising of the coins in value will cause it to be brought into the Realm from divers places in hope of gain and the debasing of the monies in the fineness and weight will keep it here for fear of loss." Maybe, some such consideration weighed with the counsellors of Henry VIII in making alteration of the coinage, when the incoming of the price revolution began to work havoc with the exchanges. We, in this age, who have experienced inflation, deflation, revaluation, and devaluation, in order to attain to a profitable level of prices, ought to be more objective in our judgment on the coinage alterations in the past.

of a certain weight had to be paid for other commodities, and conversely, in case of scarcity of money, fewer pieces of silver of the same weight were sufficient to buy other things. In the former case, it is said the things are dear, and in the latter case that things are cheap.

France, if not the first beneficiary from Spanish precious metals, was one of the first countries to which the gold and silver began to flow from Spain. French agricultural produce, finer linen and garments, were exported to the northern provinces of Spain. In the third decade it became quite noticeable. The excess of exportation was paid by Spain in precious metals. The rise of prices affected everywhere in the first place agricultural produce. French corn prices moved upwards and likewise the value of agricultural land. "In France it was observed," writes John Law in 1705, "that about two centuries ago the same land was in thirty years worth double the money it was worth before. So, land worth a 100 *lib. anno* 1500 was worth 200 *lib. anno* 1530. . . . Not the goods have risen, but the money has fallen."[1] Law's statement about the rise of agricultural land in France need not be taken as having been of general application, but as an indication of the ruling tendency of the time it is worthy of notice.

How far the French were in advance of the English as regards the influx of Spanish treasure, and consequently the price revolution, may be seen from the following comparative index figures of the price of wheat. Taking the year 1500 as representing the figure 100 the price movement of wheat in both countries was as shown in the following table:

[1] John Law, *Money and Trade*, 4th edition, 1750, p. 129.

France		England	
Price of Wheat		*Price of Wheat*[1]	
Year	*Index Figure*	*Year*	*Index Figure*
1500	100	1500	100
1501–1525	125	1501–1520	105
1526–1550	151	1521–1550	113
1551–1575	340	1551–1570	155

France, then, was much earlier and much more strongly affected by the price revolution, and it was a Frenchman, Jean Bodin, who in 1568 drew the attention of the public to the causal relation between the influx of the American treasure and the rise of prices in Europe.[2]

The influx of the West Indian precious metals affected also the ratio between gold and silver. As the latter metal came in in greater abundance than the former the traditional ratio of 10: 1 or 11: 1 changed in violent fluctuations to 12: 1, 13: 1, 14: 1, and stood in the year 1701 at 16: 1.[3]

In England the rise of prices in the home market first became noticeable from about 1540 onwards, and in a more acute form from 1570 onwards, when her merchants

[1] The tables are taken from Wiebe, *Preisrevolution im* 16 *und* 17 *Jahrhundert*, Leipzig, 1895, pp. 378–386.

[2] "Je trouve," writes Bodin, "que la cherté . . . vient quasi pour quatre ou cinq causes. La principale et presque seule (que personne jusques icy n'a pas touchée) c'est l'abondance d'or et d'argent qui est au jourdhuy en ce royaume plus grande qu'elle n'a este il y a quatre cent ans." This abundance of treasure had come from the West Indies and also from the Levant trade. (*Discours sur le rehaussement et diminution des monnoyes*, Paris, 1578.) The book has no pagination, but counting the pages from the beginning of the text the quotation is on page 13.

[3] W. A. Shaw, *Select Tracts*, ed. 1935, pp. 135, 144.

were expanding their trade into all parts of the Old World, and her seamen were capturing silver-laden Spanish galleons and planting colonies in the New World. In 1581, the anonymous editor of Hales's *Discourse* was able to point out that, next to the high rents which were the effect of the former debasement of the coinage, the abundant influx of precious metals from the Indies and other countries into England was responsible for the continuance of the dearth.[1] And the rise of prices continued well into the first decades of the seventeenth century, while in Western Germany, Flanders and France prices settled down towards the end of the sixteenth century. England was caught by the price revolution three or four decades later than France and was three decades longer under its sway than the latter. We shall learn later on how remarkable the consequences thereof were for the whole course of economic life of England from the reign of Henry VIII to that of Charles I.

5. *Delivering Money by Exchange*

The debasement of the coinage and the subsequent influx of treasure were not the only reasons brought forward as having been at the bottom of the dearth. Some mercantile writers, economists, and tradesmen of wide experience, rejected them altogether as the efficient causes of so widespread and deep disturbances. Their arguments, while differing in various respects, all centred on one and the same point—the exchanges. We shall soon hear their arguments, but in order to appreciate them, it

[1] John Hales, *A Discourse*, p. 187.

might not come amiss to say a few words about their converging point—exchanges, as then understood and reasoned upon. I shall reproduce first the definition of "exchange" as formulated by Thomas Mun (*England's Treasure*, ch. xii): "The Merchants exchange by Bills is a means and practice whereby they that have money in one country may deliver the same to receive it again in another country at certain times at rates agreed upon, whereby the lender and the borrower are accommodated without transporting treasure from State to State."

And now let me outline the business of exchange in the simplest and most salient points.

English exchange business as a separate trade goes back to the reign of Henry VII, when the vent of undyed and undressed cloth was gradually surpassing in quantity and value the export of wool. It was this growing trade which led in 1496 to the *Magnus Intercursus*—the commercial treaty between England and the Low Countries. The business accounts between English and Continental merchants could not be legally settled in coin and bullion, since the Ordinances of Bullion made sending cash abroad a felony. It was therefore necessary to find other means for that purpose, so "exchange" was introduced. For instance, when a cloth exporter in London had a certain sum of money to his credit at Antwerp and a Flemish draft for that sum, while a London importer of wine and fancy goods owed an equal sum to an Antwerp merchant, then the latter could pay to the former, that is, buy the Flemish draft, since both resided in London, and thus save the risk of sending coin or bullion abroad (i.e. the risk of loss and of contravening the Ordinances of

Bullion) and save the expenses of transport and recoinage. If the possessor of the Flemish draft was satisfied with receiving the equal sum, then the exchange was said to be at *par*. But, though such happy chances and such simplicity in doing business may have occurred in the first stage of foreign trade, later they were exceptions. The English importer of foreign goods, on having to pay to the Flemish merchant his debts or on going to Antwerp for buying goods there, had first to apply to an exchanger in Lombard Street, who dealt in such bills and who had either a factor (an agent) abroad or who enjoyed international credit and could thus draw a bill on an Antwerp banker to order of the English importer. The rates of exchange between pounds sterling and Flemish shillings varied considerably during the sixteenth and seventeenth centuries, but the rate £1=25 Flemish shillings is a good average rate, and we make it the basis of our computations.

The English importer who required, for instance, 250 Flemish pounds for the purchase of goods at the Antwerp fair might have thought that on delivering £200 he would obtain the required Flemish draft. He knew, of course, that he would have to pay a commission, amounting to about five per cent, for saving him the transport expenses, the risks of loss, and of sending cash contrary to the law, but he was at first unaware that in the exchange business the intrinsic value or standard rates of the various coins was not the decisive point. He soon learned, however, that the exchanger had, so to speak, "gone off gold" and made supply and demand the decisive factor.[1] The King's coin

[1] "These exchanges," says Thomas Mun (*England's Treasure*, ch. xii), "thus made between man and man are not contracted at the

was turned into a simple commodity, like cloth or barley, and its valuation was made by common tradespeople according to the state of the market. If Flemish bills were in strong demand, then the English importer could not get 125 Flemish pounds for his £100, but had to deliver 110 pounds sterling. The pound sterling thus fell below par: it was undervalued by ten per cent, and was not worth more than ninety pounds.

With the further growth of international commerce the importer did not deliver money but "took up" from the exchanger a draft as a loan. Credit took the place of direct payments, and the borrower was, of course, also charged with a certain rate of interest. The exchanger became an international money-lender and deliverer, and the merchant the borrower.

A bill of exchange was written as follows, assuming the name of the importer to be G. Adam, the London exchanger's Alfred Gates.

"To................Antwerp. £200 0 0

Laus Deo, 1st August, 1569, in London.

At Usance[1] pay by this Bill of Exchange unto G. Adam the summe of two hundred pounds sterling of twenty-five shillings Flemish for every pound sterling current money

equal value of moneys according to their respective weights and fineness. First, because he that delivers the money doth respect the venture of the debt, and the time of forbearance, but that which causeth an under or overvaluing of money by exchange, is the plenty or scarcity thereof in places where the exchanges are made."

[1] One month after date, "At double Usance" two months after date.

in merchandise, for value received and put it to account as per advice.

God keepe you,

Alfred Gates."

More often such a bill contained no fixed rate of exchange, but was left to the Flemish drawee to settle the rate with the English importer on his arrival in Antwerp for business. To judge from sixteenth-century documents, the importers got much the worst of their exchange bargains.

The falling exchange of sterling, once fixed and generalized, became the current rate even in markets where no sterling was due, until such a time when sterling was scarce, that is, in strong demand. It was then raised and, in its turn, overvalued. This happened when the Spaniards, who, as a rule, had to "take up" money by exchange for Bristol or London. The English exchangers undervalued the Spanish money in favour of sterling. Spain had, of course, her own bullionist laws.

Besides the form of exchange mentioned above, there were two other forms much more onerous to the "taker up." One form was "dry exchange." A merchant applied to the London banker for £100 in exchange, but the bill of exchange was not drawn to the order of the merchant, but to that of the banker's factor abroad. The merchant paid first the usual commission and brokerage to the London banker, and on arrival in Antwerp or Amsterdam he did not obtain the money from the factor, but had to take up again from him the Flemish money, and pay again brokerage, patronage, and re-change charges, and be thankful for the rate of exchange which he settled with the factor. The other form was "fictitious exchange," where the taker-up had first to feign buying commodities and, in order to pay for them, he had to take up money by exchange. According to Malynes, the merchant lost about twenty per cent in these exchanges.

Let us now return to our importer.

Casting up his accounts, he finds that his original £200 have been reduced to £170, for he paid first 5 per cent to the London exchanger for the bill, and lost also on the exchange—all on the score of the law of supply and demand.

The importer shifts his exchange losses on to the consumers, that is, he raises the price by 15 per cent, besides adding his transport and overhead expenses and the current rate of profit.

Hence the indictments against exchanges as causing the dearth.

The valuations of the exchangers, that is, their over- and undervaluations, were often arbitrary and dictated by a desire for gain, but the opportunity for such valuations was given by the balance of trade. An unfavourable balance of trade of a country resulted in an undervaluation of that country's coin, for it had to be delivered by exchange in large amounts to the exchangers or bankers, who then valued it to their own advantage.

In essence, then, it was the self-interest of the exchanger and not the intrinsic value (weight and fineness) of the coin, and still less the extrinsic value (denomination given to the coin by royal prerogative), that priced and tariffed money. To men who still cherished mediaeval views of commutative justice and iustum pretium—and there were many who still cherished them in the sixteenth and the first half of the seventeenth century—or good royalists who feared God and the King, the whole exchange business was utterly obnoxious, because sinful. They saw in it one of the main evil forces subversive of God's law, of kingship, and the whole social order. And they were not mistaken.

In the hundred years from about 1530 to 1630, and even during the Commonwealth years, the complaints against the exchangers hardly ever ceased to trouble the authorities, the economic writers, and the trading public. All economic evils were ascribed to the sinister operations of the exchangers. In the reign of Edward VI and Mary, exchangers were virtually prohibited. In the reign of Elizabeth, a tax was imposed on exchanges, and, in 1576, the mediaeval office of royal exchanger was revived. On the advice of the Keeper of the Great Seal, Sir Nicolas Bacon, Lord Treasurer, Lord Burghley, Secretary Walsingham, etc., the Queen issued a proclamation reminding all native and foreign merchants, as well as subjects of Her Majesty, that "by the lawes and statutes of this Realm no man ought to make anie exchange or rechange of money, but such as Her Majesty shall authorize to keepe, make, and answere for such exchanges and rechanges."

All those prohibitions and regulations proved, however, of no avail. The exchangers ruled the money market in Lombard Street, and the bankers at the Antwerp Bourse, and indirectly the level of prices, for, as a rule, the charges were passed on to the consumers, who had to pay higher prices.

Some writers maintained that it was the undervaluation of English money and commodities that was at the root of all the mischief from which the realm suffered. The younger generation of merchants and tradesmen, a motley crew of upstarts, having driven the old worshipful merchants out of the market, were dumping English staple commodities at low prices on the foreign markets, and buying foreign trifles, vanities, and luxuries at high prices, which then ruled the home market. The old merchants turned exchangers, buying, selling, and lending bills, and living on the gain from money, that is, "thriving on plain usury."[1]

An official report on exchanges, written in 1564, ascribed the bad economic state of England to the dishonesty, trickery, and sleight of the Antwerp exchangers, who were conspiring to bring about the ruin of England. "The Bankerers doe cunningly fall the exchange at Antwerp when foreseeing that shortely a good masse of wares wil be boughte uppe for Englande by money taken uppe by exchange. Then they forthwith take uppe all the money of the Burse to keep awhyll in their fewe handes, and within fewe dayes aftere, when the time of buyinge of ware for Englande dothe drive many to the Exchange for money to buy withall, then the Bankerers . . . may by their Conspyracye fall the price of the Exchange there to their convenient gayne."[2] The Antwerp bankers were thus raising and lowering the rate of sterling to the injury of the English trade. This was also the opinion of Guicciardini in his description of Antwerp (1567).

[1] *T.E.D.*, iii, p. 311. [2] *T.E.D.*, iii, p. 352.

6. *Gerard Malynes and Thomas Milles against Exchangers*

The most vocal and authoritative opponent of "exchange" was Gerard Malynes, an economic writer of a fairly clear English, who in the years 1600 to 1630 wrote several pamphlets and books, among them the valuable *Lex Mercatoria*, all dealing with exchange and commerce. His ancestors had their home in Lancashire, but his father, a superintendent of coinage, had emigrated to Antwerp, where Gerard was born about 1560. A year later the family returned to England, where, owing to the Elizabethan reform of the coinage, Mint masters were in demand.

There is no information about the education of the young Gerard, but, judging from his writings and from other records, he was well versed in Latin, modern languages, mathematics, and assaying. He must have learned a great deal about the commercial transactions of his time, and particularly exchange, which formed then a topic of complaints and investigations. Though half of his life was spent in the seventeenth century—he was still alive in 1641—he remained a sixteenth century man, adhering to the view that exchange of coin must be ruled by its intrinsic and extrinsic value, or *par pro pari*, and staunchly defending the monetary prerogatives of kingship.

Malynes, who for some years worked as assay master in the Mint, was often consulted on monetary and trade questions by high officials in the reign of Elizabeth and particularly in the reign of James I, who must have found in him a man after his own heart. On the other hand, he was hated by Edward Misselden, who was a member of the Merchant Adventurers, and by Thomas Mun, a member of the East India Company, and both of them protagonists of the balance of trade policy, that is, inequality of exchanges and supply and demand as the rule of economic life. Ever since 1622 they saw in Malynes a mediaeval spectre that threatened progress. Misselden dipped his pen in gall and fury, when writing against him; half of his exceedingly clever pamphlet, *Circle of Trade or Balance of Trade* (1623), is given to a refutation of Malynes's demand for *par* exchanges, and Mun devoted three chapters of his *England's Treasure* to a passionate defence of exchanges against Malynes's indictments. In justice to Mun, it must be added that he made some attempt to be fair to Malynes, of whom he writes: "I find him skilful in many things which he hath both written and collected concerning the affairs of merchants and particular he discourses well of diverse uses, forms, and passages of the exchange, in all of which he hath taken great pains for the good of others, so do his Works of this kind deserve much praise" (*England's Treasure*, ch. xiv); but he is against him on other points, charging him with selfish motives. The refutation and defence consist essentially of the argument that not the exchanger but supply and demand fixed the price of money like that of any other commodity. Mun further argued that plentifulness or scarcity of money depended on the balance of trade. If England, for instance, imported more than she exported then she would have to deliver great amounts of sterling to Holland, where, in consequence, sterling would be undervalued, and *vice versa*.

Misselden and Mun did not see that their reply was

merely begging the question. For it was exactly the law of supply and demand which Malynes held to be ethically and politically inapplicable to money. The King's coin or the money of the Commonwealth could not be turned and ought not to be turned into a source of gain. Malynes held that "money is the soul of the body commodities. It did infuse life into trafficke by the means of equalitie and equitie, thus preventing advantage between buyers and sellers."[1]

Malynes was also active in various business projects, particularly in mining silver in the North, but he failed. Mediaevalism does not agree with business, nor with government either, as Malynes's patrons, the Stuarts, had learned to their injury.

In 1600, Malynes was a member of the Commission appointed by Queen Elizabeth to investigate the causes of the money difficulties. The investigations and discussions of that Commission resulted in the view that among other considerations "the overbalancing" of imports was one of the main causes and was aggravated by the exchange operations. A year later, Malynes published his first treatise, *The Canker of England's Commonwealth*, which may be regarded as a sort of report of that Commission. His view of the economics of the sixteenth century was as follows.

The main fact was the rise of prices, which occurred without any shortage of commodities. Some thought of the enclosures as the cause: high rent, high prices of victuals, high wages of labour—hence general dearth. The merchants thought to have discovered the cause in the

[1] Gerard Malynes, *Lex Mercatoria*, 1622, p. 59.

debasement of the coinage and advised raising the price of silver in order to attract silver to the Mint and improve the standard of the coins. In the reigns of Henry VIII and Edward VI, the price of silver was actually raised from forty to sixty shillings, which could only have resulted in a further rise of the prices of commodities. Then came the influx of West Indian treasure, which further contributed to the rise of prices. At the same time, some people discovered that the prices abroad were much higher than in England. This discrepancy was due to operations of the exchangers, who, as we have shown, lowered the rate of sterling. The undervaluation of our coin had two results: first, our merchants having bought dear abroad were forced to sell dear at home. Secondly, export of specie; merchants found it profitable to defy the law and carry their coin abroad, where they could obtain for it better value. As long as merchants can exchange at par, they never transport money, but as soon as sterling falls below par, it escapes from the country. The effect is: scarcity of money at home and plenty abroad. Now, scarcity of money necessarily results in cheap prices of commodities, while the contrary takes place abroad: by reason of the plentifulness of money the prices of commodities rise there. It may, of course, be argued that if prices abroad are high, our exports ought to benefit. And so they would but for the artificial raising of the foreign money. The bankers in Antwerp or Amsterdam are raising their coin much above its standard fineness and weight, so that the foreign money brought home by our exporters can only be rechanged with a loss, which swallows all the benefit from the high foreign prices.

Exchange according to fineness has been abused, "and of late years it became, as it were, a trade in raising and falling in price, according to plentie and scarcitie of monies, and in regard to discrepancy of time and distance of time and place, (exchange) is become predominant and doth overrule the course of commodities and money, and is the very efficient cause of this overballancing of commodities." In short, the result was unequal exchanges to our injury. No wonder, then, that the realm was being impoverished. This was the canker that ate out the vitals of England's Commonwealth.

Futhermore, contrary to all precepts of Aristotle and Christian teaching, the exchangers made the coin into a merchandise and a source of gain. They usurped the prerogative of the King and made "one summe of money, of one sort and coin, having two prices and valuations at one time"—one valuation rated and tariffed "in all countries by the Prince," and the other fixed by the exchanger; this was "too high an office for subjects" to step into.[1]

A writer who worked in the same spirit as Malynes was Thomas Milles, a customs officer. His first treatise against the exchangers appeared in 1601, but there is in the British Museum only an abstract of it, published in 1619. In his *Customers Replie, or Second Apologie*, published in 1604, he declares: "Justice is distributive or commutative . . . Commutative justice encludeth traffick. The end of traffick is equalitie in supplying necessities" and excludes "private advantage" (p. 4). Milles says in his concluding chapter

[1] Gerard Malynes, *Canker of England*, 1601, pp. 34–36, 59, 63, 15, 16.

(p. 33): "That merchandising exchange is the laborinth of errors and private practice, whereby (though Kings weare crownes and seem absolutely to raigne), particular bankers, private societies of merchants and covetous persons (whose end is private gayne) are able to suspend their counsailes and controle their policies . . . lending money to Sovereigns and Emporers themselves, that onely can make coyne and should have to give largely and lende unto others. Thus making Kings to be subiects, and vassalles to be Kings."

Milles published little, for he was often employed by Secretary Walsingham in missions to France, the Low Countries, Brittany, and Scotland. He negotiated with the Scots on the Treaty of Berwick. In the parlance of to-day he might be called a high official of the Foreign Office. The Queen rewarded his services by appointing him bailiff of Sandwich, and in later years "customer" of that port, some of his duties also consisting in intercepting foreign agents and their correspondence.[1]

In his views on trade and commerce he was more thoroughgoing than Malynes. He pleaded for the revival of the Staple system, the strict enforcement of the Statutes of Employment, and an embargo on the export of coin and bullion. He regarded the whole of that body of laws as the best expression of equality and equity in economic life. Misselden declares that Malynes merely plagiarized Milles.

It was, however, Malynes who carried on the controversy about exchange. Having found that "the efficient cause" were the dishonest exchanges, Malynes recom-

[1] *Dictionary of National Biography*, sub. Milles, Thomas.

mended the re-establishment of royal control of the exchanges through appointed exchangers, whose duty would be not to allow sterling to be taken up or delivered below par. The rule to guide the exchanger should be *par pro pari*, value for value, coins to be exchanged according to their intrinsic and extrinsic value, though a certain allowance was to be made for saving risk and transport expenses. Such a par of exchanges, writes Malynes, was established in the reign of Elizabeth in 1564, 1576, 1586, 1600, "myself being a commissioner of the latter."[1]

Malynes's views are contained in his two treatises, *Canker of England's Commonwealth* (1601) and *Maintenance of Free Trade* (1622). His *Lex Mercatoria*, a large quarto volume, is a cyclopaedic collection of all the commercial knowledge of the age and a short summary of his above-mentioned two treatises: it is still valuable for economic history. All his other tracts are of less importance.

English economic science is under an obligation to Malynes, first for the term "overbalancing," which originated the idea of balance in matters of foreign trade; secondly, for laying the foundation of the quantity theory of money, which will be shewn in a later chapter; thirdly, for introducing the term "capital." The latter term, in its meaning of cash and goods in business, is to be found for the first time in his *Lex Mercatoria* (p. 363, *passim*), where he states that the ready cash and merchandise which a merchant puts into his business is called "stocke or capitall." The *Lex Mercatoria* went through six reprints in the course of the seventeenth century.

Among the statements of Malynes none is of greater

[1] Gerard Malynes, *Maintenance of Free Trade*, 1622, p. 63.

importance for our immediate purpose, that is, for the understanding of the economics of the sixteenth century, than that "some wise people, by comparing English with foreign prices, discovered that the prices abroad were higher than in England." This statement, which coincides with our statistical tables given above, finds corroboration in one of the best written papers of the middle of the sixteenth century, addressed by William Cholmley, a London cloth merchant, to the Crown. He states that "our clothe is solde to the strangers at his olde pryce, but the marchandice that cometh in is doubled." Contrary to the view of those who ascribe all the mischief to the exchangers, Cholmley points out that "the exchange doth hurt somewhat, as to say in every hundreth XXX lib., but the exalting of marchandice of foreign contreys was in every hundreth cc (200) and ccc (300), which robbyth the Realme of all the golde and sylver."[1] This is an instructive statement, which will find its interpretation in a later chapter.

7. *Excess of Imports*

As to the scarcity of money caused by an excess of imports, which made it necessary for England to "answer" or "countervail" the "overplus" by sending treasure abroad, no dissentient opinion disturbed the general concurrence of views as to the existence of the evil and its cause. It was expressed as far back as 1381 by Richard

[1] *T.E.D.*, iii, pp. 140, 146. In the middle of the sixteenth century, when Cholmley wrote his paper, the undervaluation of sterling by exchange amounted to thirty per cent.

Leye, an officer of the Mint, who publicly declared that the money was carried out of the realm "because the land spends too much in (foreign) merchandise, as in grocery, mercery, and furs."[1] In the fifteenth century the complaint regarding excessive imports of trifles, fantasies, and luxuries, found rhymed expression in *The Libelle of English Policye*:

> "Trifles, trifles that little have availed
> And things with which they featly blear our eye,
> With things not enduring that we buy;
> For much of this chaffare that is wastable
> Might be forborne for dear and deceivable."

And in 1520, in a ballad, "Nowe a Days," a writer complains:

> "Many craftesmen and halff beggars
> Both in townes and city
> French ware hither ye brought
> And Englishe handcraft gowth to nought.
> Halff this Realme, it is unwrought!
> Alas! for pure pytty."

In the following years the same complaint is voiced by Clement Armstrong, a merchant of wide experience, who animadverts: "All nacions sellyng in the countries deviseth fantasies to make Englishmen fools to get the riches owt of the realme . . . French men and others that in London sheweth ware houses full of trifles sold and bought for a hundred pounde; if the workmanship of makyng thereof taken away, the very substance beside the work is not

[1] See *supra*, VI, 6.

worth a hundred shilling."[1] About twenty years later, the inimitable Hales castigates with his gentle humour the folly of Englishmen who allow "strangers to fetche from us our great commodities for very trifles. Of the which sort I meane glasses, as well lookinge as drinckinge, as to glass windows, Dialles, tables, cardes, balles, puppetes, penhornes, inckhornes, toothpikes, gloves, knives, daggers, pouches, broches, anglets, buttons of silke and silver, erthen potes, pinnes, poyntes, hankes belles, paper, both whit and browne, and a thousand like thinges, that might either be clene spared or else made within the Realme." The development of shopkeeping in England in the first half of the sixteenth century was the marvel of all contemporary writers. "I have seen," writes Hales, "within these twenty yeres when there were not of these haberdashers . . . not a dossen in all London. And now from the Tower to Westminster alonge everie streat is full of them; and their shoppes glisters and shines . . . so to make any temperate man gaze on them and to bie somewhat, though it serve no purpose."[2]

The import of those trifles caused from time to time, when, for some reason or other, the exports failed to "answer" them, an outflow of bullion. On the occasion of an enquiry during the reign of Elizabeth into "the reasons why bullion is exported," a number of "true causes" were found, but the "causa causarum" was held to be the expenditure on "foreign commodities, because this realm spendeth more on them than the same commodities transported amount unto, as it may be perceived

[1] *T.E.D.*, iii, p. 110.
[2] John Hales, *A Discourse*, pp. 63–64.

by the wines, silkes, lawns, gold-lace, silver, lace and such like."[1]

Sir William Cecil (later Lord Burghley) warned the House of Commons that for the import of costly apparel "and other vain devices," money and treasure of the realm is and must be yearly conveyed out of the country "to answer the same excess."[2] He was pleading for the strict observance of the Sumptuary Laws. And about the year 1581, he wrote: "It is manifest that nothing robbeth the realme of England, but when more merchandises is brought into the realm than is carryed forth. If but eight hundred thousand poundes worth of forrayn commoditees be brought in, and but six hundred thousand poundes worth of the English commoditees be carryed forth, the realme must spend yerley upon the stock two hundred thousand poundes which must be payd with money, and it is manifestly scene allowedly by the customers accomptes in the exchequer that yerly the forrayn commoditees doo surmount the commoditees of the land."[3]

In order to abridge this array of evidence I shall only quote one more witness, Sir Henry Knyvet, who in debate in the House of Commons on subsidies, *anno* 1593, declared that the country was impoverished, and the "principal reason of our poverty was, because we brought in more foreign wares than we vented commodities and so by this means our money was carried out of the country, alleging it to be like a pond fed with a spring, but having a breach through which more passeth than cometh in."[4]

[1] Bland, Brown, Tawney, *Select Documents*, pp. 419–420.

[2] Strype, *Annals*, ii, p. 528.

[3] *T.E.D.*, ii, p. 124.

[4] *T.E.D.*, ii, p. 327.

The causes of the main economic phenomena of the sixteenth century were thus thought to have been—debasement of the coinage and paying high prices for silver; enclosures; ill-regulated foreign trade carried on by greedy and covetous merchants; trickery of the exchangers; under-valuation of English money by exchangers; low price of English goods; high prices of foreign goods, of which the latter were imported in excess of the value of English exports, mostly for the purpose of satisfying the craving of Englishmen for fineries, luxuries, and "belly-cheer."

8. *The Prime Cause of the Economic Difficulties*

Having heard the evidence of the most important witnesses as to the economic developments in the sixteenth century, it is time to sum up and to obtain a clear view of the whole. Until now we have been made familiar with different aspects of the price revolution. They, it is true, tell us much, but they throw light mainly on symptoms, and not on the fundamental causes that led to so many changes.

The whole set of economic phenomena in sixteenth century England may be traced back to three causes—one general, which concerned the whole of Western Europe, and two special causes, which affected England only—namely, first, the influx of West Indian silver and gold into Western and Central Europe; secondly, the relatively late participation of it by England; thirdly, the expansion of commerce and trade in England in the last decades of the sixteenth century. Let us now deal with each cause separately.

(i) The revival and growth of town life in Western Europe since the eleventh century was quickened, as already explained,[1] by the precious metals mined in Germany and by the monetary gains of the Italians in their trade with the Levant and Egypt. The cost of production or acquisition of the precious metals was relatively high, but as long as the pace of commercial development was gradual, the available monetary resources proved adequate. In the second half of the fifteenth century, however, the economic expansion began to outstrip the supply of the precious metals, so that the monetary margin proved insufficient to allow of a further development. The shortage of money manifested itself by two symptoms. The first was the general fall in prices, that is, money got dear in terms of commodities.[2] The second was the difficulty of obtaining loans, except at exorbitant rates of interest and on the best security.[3] The need for silver and gold grew all the more urgent as the trade with India, the most lucrative of all trades, was made more onerous by the triumphant Turk, who in 1453 had seized Constantinople and thus controlled both the overland and the maritime

[1] See *supra*, p. 64.

[2] The rise in the price of gold and silver in the last decades of the fifteenth century is also evident from the history of English coinage. The earliest English gold coin, weighing 128 grains, was valued at 6s. 8d. In 1489, the same valuation was set on a gold coin weighing only 80 grains. Within the same period the silver penny was reduced from 22 grains to 12 troy grains (W. A. Shaw, *History of Currency*, 1896, p. 15), this meant that in 1489, 80 grains of gold could buy the same quantity of goods as 128 grains bought in earlier times.

[3] On the general deficiency of money in Europe in the last quarter of the fifteenth century see Schanz, *Englishe Handelspolilik*, 1881, vol. i, pp. 482–486.

trade routes.[1] Those were the motives that spurred the Portuguese to continue their West African exploration and stimulated the Italians and Spaniards to embark on voyages of discovery, in which America was discovered, with the result that from about the second quarter of the sixteenth century the West Indian precious metals rolled in increasing masses into Spain and from there into Central and Western Europe. The Mexican and Peruvian silver and gold were obtained at the lowest possible cost of production (though, alas! at an appalling moral cost, which, however, does not affect trade), and could be got much cheaper than the German metals. Cheap and abundant silver meant increasingly higher prices of commodities. An upward price revolution set in, the effects of which were everywhere felt, but nobody could as yet discover its cause. That was the general cause which led to a fall in the price of silver, that is, to rising prices of commodities.

(ii) The outflow of precious metals from Spain to South Germany, France, the Low Countries, and England, was not simultaneous. France, the nearest neighbour of Spain, was affected by the influx in the third decade of the sixteenth century, partly through trading, partly through privateering, the French seamen having been the first to intercept Spanish silver and gold galleons; even the first two Spanish ships laden with Mexican silver were captured not far from the Azores by French seamen. This happened in 1522, that is, forty years before Hawkins embarked on his career. After France—perhaps at the

[1] A good description of the trade obstructions caused by the Turks is given by Thomas Mun in his *Discourse of Trade*, 1621, pp. 11–12.

same time as France—the Low Countries began to be affected. In those markets the rise of prices was soon noticeable. In England, however, the influx of the Central and South American precious metals was only started after the accession of Elizabeth. This is to say that English trade and commerce, though rapidly expanding ever since the last quarter of the fifteenth century, were still moving on a narrow metallic basis, the cost of production of which was comparatively high. Money was relatively scarce[1] and, therefore, the price level low. English exporters sold cheap and English importers bought dear, that is, at prices ruling in France or the Low Countries, which possessed an abundance of precious metals at a low cost of production. Hence the periodic outflow of gold and silver to "answer" the "overplus" of payments for imports, and which in the decades between 1530 and 1570 caused at certain periods a money scarcity. For we must not assume that the losing game was going on steadily during the greater part of the sixteenth century. English trade had among the Merchant Adventurers business men of international experience, and among the London merchants excellent financiers, such as Sir Thomas Gresham, who saw to it that the Flemish, French, and Germans should not enjoy the full benefit of their monetary advantages. But how are we to account for the fact that even in the last quarter of the sixteenth century, when the inaugurated protectionist policy fostered trade and when the influx of West Indian precious metals did finally reach England,[2]

[1] English monarchs—Henry VIII, Edward VI, Elizabeth (in the first years of her reign)—raised loans, not at home, but in Flanders.

[2] John Hales, *A Discourse*, p. 187; W. Harrison, *A Description of England*, pp. 238–243.

the complaints about money scarcity did not cease, and apparently with good reason, for there is sufficient evidence that large enterprises were suffering from money difficulties, so that, as mentioned before, Queen Elizabeth, in 1600, appointed a commission to investigate the causes thereof.[1] And here we come to the treatment of the third cause, which should throw light on the economic conditions of the last decades of sixteenth-century England.

(iii) Since about 1570, the expansion of manufacture, mining, shipping, and the general commercial activities of the various trading companies, were making demands upon the available treasure to which it was by no means equal. Under the pressure of the economic expansion and its urge for money, the mediaeval usury laws fell (1571), and

[1] *Calendar of State Papers, Domestic*, No. 121, pp. 47–48. Some writers are inclined to make light of the complaints about money scarcity and think them to be no more than the usual croakings of farmers and business people about bad trade. This is not my opinion, for there is evidence that they contained much truth and they were voiced also by economic writers and public men. Here is some of the evidence. In the debate of the Commons in March 1593 on Queen Elizabeth's request for three subsidies, Francis Bacon declared that they could not be paid in less than six years, else the gentlemen would have to sell their plate and the farmers their brass pots. The same debate, at which several speakers complained that at the preceding assessments for a subsidy some London merchants were unjustly favoured, brought out statistics of the incomes of the London merchants about the year 1590.

In the wealthiest city of the Kingdom there were at that time four persons with incomes of £400 each; eighty persons with £300–£350; thirty-two persons with £200–£250; hundred and forty-eight persons with £100–£180; five hundred and four persons with £50–£90 each. No wonder that even the East India Company had to struggle with financial difficulties. At the first voyage equipped by the Company (1601), several members failed to pay up their quota and the contributions to the expenses fell short by £8,000–£9,000. There is also some evidence that mining operations had to be stopped owing to shortage of money.

plans were suggested for the establishment of a public bank.[1] Scarcity of money, then, meant in those years, not a relative diminution of the wealth of the country, but shortage of the monetary stock, or what became known later on as capital, that was required for the opening up and financing of new material resources and the extension of old ones. The merchants were assimilating the lesson taught by mercantilist writers about the wealth that would accrue to them from the export of manufactured commodities and from shipping, and they were establishing manufactories for producing those goods which they used to import from abroad. They extended coal mining and iron founding, searched for copper and zinc, built ships, manufactured glass and paper, improved the methods of beer, spirits, and sugar production, and they were above all eager to obtain highly skilled foreign clothiers, dyers, and miners. Still, with the exception of Newcastle coal mining and some Sussex ironworks, in which much money was sunk, it was mostly done on a modest scale. In those years, merchants reckoned, at the highest, with thousands of pounds, and not with ten thousands, let alone hundred thousands. None the less, it may be safely asserted that in the last decades of the sixteenth century the English middle class started on its manufacturing and maritime career.

We can see now that the embarrassments and disadvantages—rise of prices and scarcity of money—under which sixteenth-century England laboured, were due neither to the wickedness nor the greed of the merchants, nor to the debasement of the coinage, nor to the trickery

[1] *State Papers, Domestic: Elizabeth*, vol. cx, No. 57.

and conspiracy of the exchangers, but to economic developments in Western Europe in general and England in particular. The desire for gain—the main motive of the economic man—the utilization of the chances which economic life offered, if practised regardless of the common interests, undoubtedly aggravated the effects of the monetary developments, but were not their principal cause. The exchanger raised and lowered the rate of the monetary units; the traders took advantage of the rising market and raised prices; the dealer in money exported English gold to markets, where, in consequence of the influx of West Indian precious metals, the ratio between gold and silver moved in violent fluctuations from the traditional 10: 1 or 11: 1 to 12: 1, 13: 1, 14: 1, and thus offered opportunities for profitable arbitrage; finally, those who possessed silver did not bring it to the Mint whenever the market rate was above the Mint rate, thus causing a temporary scarcity of coin. All those opportunities and activities, however, were but the effects of the three causes mentioned above.

The fact that the contemporaries ascribed their troubles to the depravity of certain persons need not to be wondered at. It is so much easier to find scapegoats among an unpopular class of men—and the merchants and exchangers were then very unpopular—than to find the efficient cause in a bewildering multiplicity of economic and social phenomena. Had there been Jews in London in those times, the finding of scapegoats would have been easier still. There existed during the greater part of the sixteenth century not a single economic writer or moral philosopher who grasped the prime cause that was operating in the upward drive of the price revolution. Nobody was able to see as yet that the large masses of Mexican and Peruvian gold and silver, obtained at bare transport cost, that is, at an incomparably lower production cost than the German metals, in their impact on the narrow monetary basis of the European economic system, destroyed the equilibrium of exchanges. And still less was any English economic writer or merchant able to discover or appreciate the fact that the influx of the West Indian gold and silver reached the English shores about forty years later than it reached France and the Low Countries. In consequence of that fact, the French and the Flemish trade throve on an abundance of cheap money, as trade is always thriving on a rising market, while English trade suffered periodically from a stringency of money, which meant a low price level. The English merchant, therefore, often sold cheap, but had to buy dear.

All the evils that English sixteenth-century writers complain of flowed from these three causes.

9. *The Quantity Theory of Money: John Locke*

The reflections and discussions caused by the alteration or debasement of the coinage in connection with the "dearth" resulted in the view, expressed by Hales, that it was not the royal stamp or denomination, but the metallic substance, the gold and silver, that made money valuable. The precious metals, on account of their use (utility) and rarity, were valuable and gave value to money, which measured the value of the commodities.

This was a revolutionary pronouncement, for it ran

full tilt at the sacred prerogative of the King concerning the valuation of money. It was a pronouncement the subversive effect of which can only be realized by those who have fully entered into the spirit that pervaded the atmosphere of the period, in which the "most dreade majesty" of personal monarchy ruled supreme.

The first step was thus taken towards a theory of money—a step which left behind the schoolmen's view that money was merely a conventional measure of value or price. It was a break with mediaevalism.

A further step in the same theoretical direction was taken in consequence of the influx from the West Indies of large masses of cheaply obtained precious metals and its effect on the movement of prices. Writers on economic questions finally found that it was the large increase of gold and silver that caused the revolutionary rise in prices. This meant that more grains of gold and silver had to be given for the same quantity of commodities than before: commodities became dearer because the precious metals became cheaper. Gold and silver, being commodities like any other commodities, were likewise subject to supply and demand, or, as it was expressed in those times, plentifulness made them good cheap, scarcity made them dear. Prices of commodities depended, then, not only on their own plenty or scarcity, but also on the quantitative supply of currency, that is, on the quantity of precious metals that are available for commerce. This conclusion laid the foundation for the quantity theory of money, and it was gradually developed in the course of the seventeenth century.

The first empirical and tentative expression of the

quantity theory of money is to be found in Malynes's writings. "Plenty of money maketh generally things dear, and scarcity of money maketh likewise generally things good cheap. Whereas things particularly are also dear or good cheap according to plenty or scarcity of the things themselves, or the use of them."[1]

The effect of the available quantity of money on prices became gradually a commonplace, so that Thomas Mun could write: "It is a common saying that plenty or scarcity of money makes all things dear or good cheap" (*England's Treasure*, ch. 5). In the course of the seventeenth century it came to be realized that the value of money or the price of commodities depended on a certain proportion which the currency bears to the available commodities. If the quantity of current money is increased while the quantity of commodities remained stationary a rise of prices was inevitable, and, conversely, if the quantity of commodities increased while the quantity of currency remained stationary or decreased, a fall of prices was inevitable. The economic writers, who in those times pleaded for the creation of paper money, were met with the objection that such a measure would merely cause a rise of prices "proportionably to such increase of money."[2]

The first clear enunciation of the essence of the quantity theory of money was given by the anonymous author of *Britannia Languens*, who wrote in the years between 1676–1680. He declared: "If there were but 500 l. sterling in England, an ox could hardly be worth a penny, nor

[1] Gerard Malynes, *Canker of England*, 1601, p. 10. *Id. Centre of the Circle of Commerce*, 1623, p. 14.

[2] William Potter, *Key to Wealth*, 1650, p. 13.

could the revenue of all England be above 500 l. sterling per annum."[1]

A clearer, but much later, exposition of that theory was given by Richard Cantillon. "Suppose," he writes, "a town and the lands about it have no communication with their neighbours, and that the money in circulation is £100,000 to carry on all its wants, and let it be supposed that this sum is somehow increased to £200,000, such a town and its districts would not be richer, happier, or more powerful than before, but the price of things would be double to what they were before."[2]

A more concise formulation of that theory was given by John Locke in 1692: "The value of money in general is a quantity of the current money in that country in proportion to the present trade . . . The quantity of money that is necessary to drive trade, that is, to carry goods from the producer to the consumer, determines its value." Locke admits that it is difficult to determine the adequate proportion of current money, for the rapidity of circulation of the money differs greatly; where the circulation is rapid a relatively small quantity of money will move a large quantity of commodities. A shilling which changes hands in the market twenty times during a single day will drive as much trade as £1 which changes hands only once. The quantity theory of money is thus modified by the pace of the circulation of money.

This theory, as formulated by Locke, is not the whole truth. We must not be carried away by the reputation of

[1] *Britannia Languens,* 1680, p. 8 (in McCulloch's *Early English Economic Tracts,* p. 290).

[2] Richard Cantillon, *Analysis of Trade,* London, 1759, pp. 30–31.

Locke as a great philosopher. For in economics he was but an eclectic, combining mechanically Aristotelian and scholastic teaching with doctrines of mercantilism as he found them. With Locke as an economist we shall deal later on. Meanwhile we may remark that he failed to take into account the main factor of value—namely, cost of production. He was far behind Sir William Petty, who in 1662, in his *Treatise of Taxes*, gave to the world the first objective theory of value and money, as shown in a later chapter.

It was said above that the quantity theory of money contained a certain measure of truth, but it required some qualification. It arose at a time when traffic and commerce, that is, the circulation of goods, were thought to be the main source of obtaining treasure, and the flow of the precious metals was interfered with and made difficult owing to legal measures and bullionist prohibitions. It was essentially an interpretation and generalization of two conditions in early modern times—namely, the prevalence of bullionist prohibitions and the price revolution caused by the influx of large quantities of West Indian metals. The generalization is faulty, for it considered only the quantitative increase of metals, without having regard to the fact that their cost of production was incomparably lower than that of the German metals. Not only the abundance of precious metals, but also their low cost of production told on the movement of prices. It practically operated like a paper money inflation with a very slender covering of commodity values.[1] As a matter of fact, the

[1] As an interesting sidelight on the gold and silver inflation the following may serve: "The Historie of the West Indies maketh mention," writes Malynes (*England's View*, 1603, pp. 9–10), "that during

German mines had soon to stop working on account of the West Indian competition.[1] The quantity theory of money, then, is valid only under certain circumstances, that is, where and when the supply and circulation of money is restricted or inhibited, but, on the whole, it is only subsidiary to the general theory of money.

the great quantitie or abundance of gold and silver that was found about fourscore years past, and the rareness of other things, a cloak of cloth was sold in Peru for a thousand duckets, a paire of breaches of cloth for three hundred duckets, a good horse foure or five thousand duckets, and other things then in use and rare accordingly."

A very similar state of things prevailed in Germany in the worst inflation year, 1923, but the "abundance" was, of course, not in gold and silver—it was all paper.

[1] It was this competition that caused the decline of the famous South German commercial houses, the Fuggers and the Welsers, whose fortunes had been built up on gold and silver mining.

VIII

BALANCE OF TRADE

1. *Mediaeval and Modern Conception of Trading*

The opinion generally held in the latter half of the sixteenth century that the excess of imports, by causing an outflow of English treasure, was impoverishing the realm, easily suggested the remedy. It was but necessary to reduce the "overplus" in order to balance imports and exports. Yet opinions differed as to the remedial measures. And the difference of opinion is very characteristic and instructive. It was a clash between lingering mediaeval ethics and modern wealth acquisition practice, that is, the rise of the "economic man."

Aristotle (*Politics*, I, 3, §§ 6–21) remarks that there are two ways in trading—one of the *Oekonomikos* or the *Politikos*, the head of a household or the head of a state, whose trading has for its purpose the satisfaction of the wants of the family or of the citizens of the state; the other way of trading Aristotle calls chrematistic (in the language of the schoolmen, *ars pecuniativa* or *ars acquirendi*), that is, money-getting is its aim. The answer of the sixteenth-century England to the question of regulating trade with a view to preventing scarcity of money was likewise two-fold. The scholars and high state officials, guided by the mediaeval principal of commutative justice, were for the establishment of a certain harmony between imports and exports: not to buy more than we sell. This was the answer of John Hales, Thomas Milles, Sir William Cecil, and the high dignitaries of King James I—quite in the spirit of the advice of the five Mint officers (Lye, Aylesbury, etc.) in 1381–1382. We have in an earlier chapter referred to the opinion of the latter, as well as to those of Milles and Hales (though, as pointed out, Hales was not consistent).

Of no less importance is the opinion of Sir William Cecil (Lord Burghley). About the year 1564 he wrote a "memorandum" on the export trade, in which he warned the country that the realm "is overburdened with unnecessary forrayn wares, and if the trade thereof shall contynew but a whyle, a great part of the tresor of the money of the realme would be carryed thither to answer for such unnecessary triffles." About the year 1581, Lord Burghley again deplored the excess of imported merchandise, "that robbeth the realm of England" of its treasure for "the forrayn commodities doo surmount the commodities of the land." What remedy did the statesman propose? In both cases he strongly recommended to "abridge the use of such forrayn commodities as be not necessary for use," that is, to observe the Sumptuary Laws concerning "apparell and taverns for excessyve abundance of wynes."[1]

Finally, I may refer to the instruction given in 1622 by the semi-mediaeval King James I to the Commission on Trade. The Commission consisted of fifty-one members, the great majority of whom were high state dignitaries and noblemen, among them being Viscount Mandeville,

[1] *T.E.D.*, ii, pp. 45, 124.

Lord President of the Privy Council, Earl of Northampton, Lord President of the Council, two Lord Presidents of Wales and the "North Parts," Sir Julius Cesar, Master of the Rolls, Sir Robert Cotton, etc. There were also a few representatives of trade and commerce, among them Sir Dudley Digges and Thomas "Monne" (Mun), both members of the East India Company. The Commission had to review the whole economic life, and they were also asked, "diligently to observe the true ballance of the trade" and to consider measures to reduce the imports "to equalitie" with the exports.[1] They were not asked to consider measures to cause exports to exceed imports, but to obtain "the true ballance of the trade"—namely, equality of exchanges. In short, the remedy was harmonizing imports with exports through moderation and restraint, that is, through ethical behaviour.

Quite different was the remedy proposed by the merchants. It was not sufficient to countervail the imports by exports, for, as the results of the whole bullionist legislation had shown, equality of exchanges brought no gain,[2] while the merchants were in urgent need of monetary stock for their expanding commerce and manufactures. Traffic should, therefore, be used to enrich the country, and this could only be achieved at the expense of the foreigner. Trade should be so regulated as always to get

[1] Rymer-Sanderson, *Foedera*, vol. xvii, p. 413. The instruction is extensive; it takes twelve folio columns.

[2] The mercantilist doctrine supposes that "when two places trade with one another, if the balance be even, neither of them either loses or gains; but if it leans in any degree to one side, that one of them loses, and the other gains" (Adam Smith, *Wealth of Nations*, iv, ch. 3).

an excess of exports over imports, since it is "an unfailing rule that the excess must be brought in in gold and silver," the universal embodiments of wealth.

Ever since the middle of the sixteenth century the teachings of the Fathers, Greek philosophers, and Canonists on trade and usury were being discarded in favour of the Roman commercial rules, the most drastic expression of which was Marcus P. Cato's advice to the husbandman to sell all he could and buy as little as possible; he should even sell his worn-out cattle and aged slaves, for "opportet patrem familias vendacem esse, non emacem"—it behoves the husbandman to be a seller and not a buyer (*De Agricultura*, II). This saying of the Roman economic man became one of the most favoured stock-phrases. It was quoted even in the House of Commons.

Let me reproduce one of the most characteristic passages in support of the above statement. John Stow, in his *Survey of London* (1598), reprinted a very interesting paper, written by a London merchant, under the title *An Apologie (or Defence) of the Cittie of London*, against its detractors, who thought that the city was not doing its duty towards the realm. It was written about the year 1578 and it declares, "For seeing wee have no way to encrease our treasure by mines of gold and silver at home and can have nothing without money or ware from other countries abroad, it followeth necessarily that if wee follow the counsel of that good olde husband Marcus Cato, saying, 'Opportet patrem familias vendacem esse non emacem,' and do carrie more commodities in value over the seas then wee bring hether from hence, that then the Realme shall receive that overplus in money."[1]

One of the first representatives of the chrematistic way, which became later known as the balance of trade policy, was thought to be a certain Clement Armstrong, who, writing at latest in 1535, demands "that the holl welthe of the realme is for all our riche commodities to get out of all other reamys therefore redy money, so shall all peple in the realme be made riche therewith . . . What English merchantes carrieth out of Englande to more value, then they must therefore bring gold and silver . . . By such an ordre Englande by Goddes grace may shortely be made a rich realme."[2]

Then we have a very entertaining treatise, entitled *Policies to Reduce this realme of Englande unto a prosperus wealthe and estate*, written in 1549. The anonymous author is a determined Protestant, rejoicing that the true faith would enable Englishmen to introduce good statutes to "reforme those inconveniences which tende . . . unto the utter desolation of the Realme." The common people must be set to work, so that England should be able to export annually goods to the value of twelve-hundred thousand pounds, instead of six hundred thousand pounds as hitherto. It could be done, considering that in the recent past "a great nombre of Monkes, Channons, Friars, and Chantrye priestes with their Servantes were mayntayned in Idelness; when the Abbeys dyd stande; and the realme did also bestow them in Idelness and Idell workes in gooing of pilgrimagis,

[1] John Stow, *Survey of London*, ed. Kingsford, 1908, vol. ii, p. 210.

[2] *T.E.D.*, iii, pp. 105, 129.

keeping of Idell holly days: Carvinge, paintinge and gilding of Imagis, and yet the artificers and laborers in those dayes did all the worke . . . for the tilling and manuring and for the victualling and clothing all the people in the holl realme." The superfluous holidays should be abolished. "For there is yet standing beside the Sundays thirty-five hollidays, whereof twenty-five may be well put downe." Artificialte should be protected by high import duties and exports promoted. For "it is an infallible argument that if we sende yerely into beyond the Sees one hundrethe thousande poundes worthe of wares more then we receive yerely agane, then must ther nedes be brought unto this realme for the saide hundrethe thousande poundes worthe of wares so muche in value either of golde or sylver." And again, "The onlie meanes to cause muche bullione to be brought oute of other realmes unto the kinge's mintes is to provide that a great quantitie of our wares maye be carriede yerely into beyonde the Sees and lesse quantitie of their wares be brought hither agene. For if it so were that we did sende thither yerely in wares the value of six hundrethe thousande poundes and receve agene no wares from them, no man can then deny but we should receve from thence yerely in bullion or in our own coyne the value of the saide six hundrethe thousande pounds."[1]

In a *Memorandum prepared for the Royal Commission on the Exchange*, 1564, it is declared, "The cheefeste and the most proffytable remedy is to governe this Realme by good pollecy in such temperate soarte that the strange wares vented into this Realme yearly maye be of lesse

[1] *T.E.D.*, iii, pp. 318, 321.

vallewe than our Englishe wares yearly vented out of the Realme shall amount unto . . . The overvallue of our Englishe wares will yearly bringe in Emporyall and French Crownes, for they are corrante heare, whereby this Realme shall be enriched."[1]

Finally, William Lane, a London merchant, writing to Sir William Cecil, reiterates the general complaint that "the bringing in of superfluous commodities, do exsede in valewe the rychness of our commodity," was impoverishing the realm; he therefore proposes, that it should be "broughte to passe that the commodytys of owre Realme and the travyll of owre pepull solde in forin contres maye exsede in valewe the foreign commodytys broughte in, and so much shall owr commonwelthe be yerely gainers of them, and they not of us, and we to lyve off them and they not off us, and owre Reme so much inrychyd with their money and also keepe owre coyne still."[2]

2. *Rise of the term "Balance of Trade"*

Out of the proposals of the merchants, and not of those of the scholars and statesmen, arose the balance of trade doctrine. The term was gradually evolved in the first fifteen years of the seventeenth century.

The terms "balancing" and "balance" were known to book-keepers in the second half of the sixteenth century. They signified "reckoning" up the columns debitor and creditor and bringing "concordance" between them. In that sense they are used by John Mellis, a schoolmaster in Southwark, in his *Briefe Instruction and Manner how to*

[1] *T.E.D.*, iii, p. 353. [2] *T.E.D.*, ii, pp. 184–185.

keepe books of Accounts after the order of Debitor and Creditor. The booklet was published in 1588 and is still worth reading by economic historians. There is no pagination, but short numbered chapters. The above-mentioned terms are to be found in chapters 10, 21, 22. Mellis knew also the term "capital," but only in the sense of a stock of commodities, with the exclusion of money, which, in book-keeping, Mellis called Capsa, a chest. Capsa and capital formed two opposite columns.

It is probably from book-keeping that those terms were transferred to mercantilist writings, since up to the middle of the seventeenth century mercantilist writers were merchants.

As mentioned in a previous chapter, Queen Elizabeth appointed in 1600 a commission to enquire into the money difficulties of the realm. The commission consisted of Alderman Sir Richard Martin and eleven other members, among them Gerard Malynes. In the spring of 1601, the commission reported that the cause of the large export of treasure and smaller import thereof was due to: (i and ii) overheaviness of the gold coin and overrichness of the other coins; (iii) disproportion of the value of our gold and silver (our ratio being 11: 1 and abroad 12: 1); (iv) overbalancing of imports above our exports; (v) abuse of exchange between us and other nations; (vi) neglect of home manufacture. "Touching the abuse of exchange, which rises and falls according to the plenty and scarcity of money, we find that when the price of exchange is low here, so that more will be given for our money in specie than can be had for it beyond the seas by bill of exchange, then our monies are exported. It is also thought that by this abuse of the exchange exports must decrease and imports will increase. As for remedies, some think that the exchange for all places to be kept at a certainty, according to the value of the coin current. For the redress of excessive imports, we think that the Statute of Employment should be put in execution."[1]

The full term "balance of trade," however, appears to have been employed for the first time in 1615. In that year two customs officers, Sir Lionel Cranfield and Sir John Wolstenholme, reported on the export and import of the preceding ten years. Cranfield's report was endorsed on May 21, 1615, with the following words: "Sir Lionel Cranfield his Ballance of Trade."[2]

In 1616, Francis Bacon, in a paper entitled "Advice to Sir George Villiers" (Duke of Buckingham), wrote: "Let the foundation of profitable trade be thus laid that the exportation of home commodities be more in value than the importation of foreign, so we shall be sure that the stocks of the Kingdom shall yearly increase, for the balance of trade must be returned in money or bullion."[3]

In the Instruction of James I, given in 1622 to the Commission on Trade, there occurs, as mentioned in the preceding chapter, the term "the true ballance of the trade" as meaning equalizing imports with exports.[4]

[1] *Calendar of State Papers, Domestic Series*, No. 121, pp. 47–48.

[2] British Museum, Lansdowne MSS., vol. 152, fols. 175–186, 196.

[3] Francis Bacon, *Works*, ed. Spedding, Ellis, Heath, 1872, vol. xiii, p. 22.

[4] Rymer-Sanderson, *Foedera*, first edition, vol. xvii, pp. 410–415. Researches on the origin of the term "Balance of Trade" were first made by W. H. Price, and the results published in the *Quarterly Journal of Economics*, Cambridge, Mass., 1905.

The difference between the meaning of the balance of trade in Bacon's "Advice" and that in the Instruction of the advisers of King James, is a further confirmation of my differentiation between the attitude of merchants and high state officials regarding the course of international commerce. Bacon, the anti-mediaeval philosopher, mercantilist, and pioneer of the application of science to manufactures, was, as we have seen, for overbalancing exports; the advisers of King James were for equality of exchanges.

The document of 1615, with the term "balance of trade," is still extant in manuscript. Bacon's "Advice" to the Duke of Buckingham was not published before 1661. The Instruction to the commission in 1622 was, as far as I know, only published by Rymer-Sanderson (1717), so that the priority of having published the term "balance of trade" must be given to Edward Misselden, whose *Circle of Commerce or Ballance of Trade* was printed in 1623.

It was, however, Bacon who in the third edition of his *Essays* (1625) popularized the idea among the public at large. Only a very limited circle of merchants read or knew of Misselden, while all Englishmen who could read knew Bacon's *Essays*. In the essay "Of Seditions and Troubles," he writes: "The first remedy or prevention, is to remove by all means possible that material cause of sedition, which is want and poverty in the estate. To which purpose serveth the opening and well balancing of trade; the cherishing of manufactures; the banishing of idleness." In the next paragraph he proceeds to explain the meaning of it. "It is likewise to be remembered that for as much as the increase of any estate must be upon the foreigner, for whatsoever is somewhere gotten is somewhere lost, there can be but three things which one nation selleth into another; the commodity as nature yieldeth it; the manufacture and the vecture or carriage. . . . And it comes many times to pass that *materiam superabit opus*, that the work and carriage is more worth than the material, and enricheth a state more."

Bacon also enunciated the balance of power policy. In the essay "Of Empire," he writes, "Princes do keep due sentinel that none of their neighbours do overgrow so by increase of territory, by embracing of trade . . . that they become more able to annoy them. . . . During that triumvirate of Kings—King Henry the Eighth, of England; Francis the First, King of France; and Charles the Fifth, emperor, there was such a watch kept that none of the three could win a palm of ground, but the other two would straightways balance it, either by confederation or if need were, by war."

Some years later Thomas Mun wrote his *England's Treasure by Forraign Trade*, with the supplementary title "or the Ballance of Forraign Trade the Rule of our Treasure," but it was only published in 1664. One year earlier (1663), Samuel Fortrey published his very interesting treatise, *England's Interest and Improvement*, of which he says in the preface that it contained nothing which any educated person did not already know, and he deals with the balance of trade as a subject with which merchants were quite familiar. "If by right ordering and disposing of our trade our exportations did exceed our importations in value, our coin and bullion would be daily increased; there being no other means to even the balance of trade."[1]

The formulation of this policy is contained in Thomas Mun's above-mentioned treatise. There might be, Mun admitted, some other ways to get treasure into the Kingdom, but they were all either uncertain or of little importance. "The ordinary means therefore to increase our wealth and treasure is by forraign trade, wherein we must ever observe the rule to sell more to strangers yearly than wee consume of their in value. For suppose that when this Kingdome is plentifully served with the cloth, lead, tinn, iron, fish and other native commodities, we doe yearly export the overplus to forraign countries to the value of twenty two hundred thousand pounds, by which means we are enabled beyond the seas to buy and bring in forraign wares for our use and consumptions to the value of twenty hundred thousand pounds; by this order duly kept in our trading, we may rest assured that the kingdom shall be enriched yearly by two hundred thousand pounds, which must be brought to us in so much treasure; because that part of our stock which is not returned to us in wares must necessarily be brought home in treasure" (ch. 2).

Mun maintains that if we bought less from the foreigner than we sold to him we shall be enriched by the balance, for only that treasure remains actually in the country which we obtain by the yearly balance of trade. He is in that treatise against the Statutes of Employment, against

[1] Sam Fortrey, *England's Interest and Improvement*, 1663, ed. Hollander, p. 31. This treatise was highly thought of by Sir William Petty and Josiah Child.

all restrictions of money exportation, and he makes a valiant attempt to show "the order and means whereby we may draw up a balance of our foreign trade" (ch. 20), but he only shows how difficult it was to obtain a reliable account of the exports and imports.

Owing to the absence of trade statistics and the inefficiency of the customs service, all accounts of the foreign trade of those times are no more than rough computations arrived at by multiplying the customs receipts by twenty. Mun himself shows in the chapter referred to above how unreliable and misleading those computations were: "For in this manner (of computations) the 10,000 bags of pepper which we brought in this year from the East Indies should be valued at very near 250,000 pounds, whereas all this pepper . . . cost not above 50,000 pounds."

The following facts may further illustrate the difficulties and uncertainties of all attempts at obtaining reliable information about the course of trade. In 1615, Sir Lionel Cranfield, Surveyor-General of Customs, and his assistant, Sir John Wolstenholme, were instructed to report on the foreign trade of the ten years 1605–1611. Their computations were based on the identical table of customs inward and outward received by the various customs houses in those ten years. Yet the results at which each arrived differed widely from one another. In the last quarter of the seventeenth century, Sir Charles Davenant, Commissioner of Excise, proved by statistical figures that in the years from 1656 to 1688 England's wealth steadily increased, and about the year 1688 it increased by two millions annually (*Works*, vol. i, p. 93). The author of *Britannia Languens*, p. 108 (390), proved statistically that in the years from 1657 to 1675, English treasure decreased by over five millions. John Pollexfen, Commissioner of Trade and Plantations, writing against Davenant, computed that England grew poorer by £400,000 annually.[1] In a later chapter this problem is dealt with in connection with the writings of Sir Josiah Child, Nicholas Barbon, etc.

Some writers believed the rate of exchange at sterling to be the best indication of the balance of trade. If the rate was against sterling then England was losing in the balance, and *vice versa*. But the fluctuations in the values of moneys were so continuous a phenomenon that no inferences could be safely drawn from them regarding the economic condition of any country.

Those defects, however, did not in the least impair the effectiveness of the doctrine, for it implied much more than annual trade balances. It was the war-cry of the merchants in their struggle for the control of trade.

3. *Origin of Some Ideas of the Balance of Trade*

Apart from the supreme importance attached in mercantilist times to treasure, which I believe has been satisfactorily dealt with in former chapters, the balance of trade doctrine contains two ideas that offer difficulties to the modern mind. First, that only foreign trade can enrich the country; secondly, that trade within the home country is a mere transfer or conveyance of goods from one person to another, without benefiting the country as a whole.

These ideas were held by all great mercantilists, though

[1] John Pollexfen, *England and East India*, 1697, p. 6–9.

since the end of the seventeenth century contradictory views were being thrown into discussion.

On closer examination we shall find that those ideas arose naturally, that is, with economic necessity, out of the effects of the Statutes of Employment. According to those statutes the foreign importers, having paid their inward customs and disposed of their goods, could not get away with the proceeds of their sales, but were bound to lay out their money in English goods, and on leaving the country with them pay outward customs. From the point of view of the English merchant, the whole transaction reduced itself to barter, the only beneficiary being the King, who got his customs, subsidies, impositions, etc., a part of which was most probably paid by the English consumer. The treasure of the trading community did not undergo any change. There was but an exchange of goods of equal value.

To illustrate these transactions let us assume that Flemish, French, and Italian merchants imported goods to England to the value of £500,000, including charges and profit. They paid *ad valorem* customs of about 20 per cent, that is £100,000. They sold their goods for £600,000, and received the money. As they could not carry it out of the country they had to buy English goods, some of which they needed and gladly bought, while other English goods they needed less, but could not help buying and were, so to speak, thrust upon them at a low price. The English trading community, if it actually lost nothing in these transactions, also gained nothing. Its stock of treasure suffered no change for the better. It was, to be sure, an equality of exchanges according to commutative justice, but trade could not prosper on it, the country could not be enriched by selling and buying in the home market, for such transactions were tantamount to a mere transfer of goods from one set of persons to another.

Quite different was the position when the English merchant exported either his staple commodities or re-exported some of the imported French or Italian goods to Spain, the Levant, or Eastern European countries. In such exports he obtained treasure and if his sales in foreign markets amounted to a larger sum than he bought there, the surplus or the balance of the trade was necessarily brought home in treasure and the country was by so much the richer.

The experience gathered in the three centuries of the rule of the employment statutes gradually crystallized into the ideas that were embodied in the doctrine of the balance of trade. And owing to that experience the merchants set their face against equality of exchanges. They arrived at the conclusion that the injunction "not to buy more than we sell" must be superseded by the rule to buy less than we sell, as that wise husbandman Marcus Cato taught us. One has only to read and ponder chapter 10 of Thomas Mun's *England's Treasure* in order to see the effect of the statutes of employment on trade. Its heading says all there is to be said about it. It runs as follows: "The observation of the statute of employments to be made by strangers, cannot encrease nor yet preserve the treasure."

4. *Thomas Mun and Edward Misselden*

In point of character and achievement there was considerable difference between Thomas Mun, Gerard Malynes, and Edward Misselden, the three contemporary merchant-writers who filled the stage of mercantilist controversy in the two decades that preceded and, in the economic sphere, adumbrated the Civil War.

Malynes was armed with the knowledge of the materials and forms of international trade of his age, but rather as a teacher and professional writer than a practical merchant. His commercial activities were combined with his self-imposed mission to uphold and spread the principles laid down by Aristotle, the schoolmen, and the statutes concerning bullion and merchant-strangers, that is, that money was a measure of value to equalize the exchange of commodities and that it was unjust to make coin an object of gain; further, that the valuation of money was a royal prerogative, and that the statutes of employment should be strictly observed. To most readers Malynes will probably appear hopelessly mediaeval, but he did not appear so in the first decades of the seventeenth century.[1] Moreover, we shall soon learn that Mun himself was in 1621 in favour of the statutes of employment and he complained also about the abuse of exchanges, and that Misselden differed only from Malynes on the question of *par pro pari* in money exchanges. The crisis in their views came in 1623, as will be presently shown.

Misselden was a learned merchant of an ambitious,

[1] Even as late as 1640 a writer on money, a member of Gray's Inn, declared that "exchange is mixed with an usury of place as well as of time" (Rice Vaughan, *Of Coin and Coinage*, p. 10).

scintillating, intellectual type, as much eager to provoke as to face opposition. It must have been very stimulating to have a talk with him. He could quote Greek and Latin, Hebrew and Rabbinic, and he took pleasure in displaying the jewels of his astonishingly wide scholarship on the foil of his opponent's alleged ignorance. He came from a family of moneyers and merchants, who, like the Mun family, resided in Hackney. He joined early the Merchant Adventurers, the oldest and wealthiest trading company, but at that time visibly in decline. In 1623, Misselden entered also the service of the East India Company, the rising star on the horizon of English commerce. He thus came into contact with Thomas Mun, one of the most prominent members of that Company.

Mun was a merchant pure and simple, with no claim to scholarship, though he knew Latin and advised his son to learn the Latin tongue. He and Misselden took to authorship from the same occasion. From about 1620 the position of the English export trades deteriorated. There was scarcity of money and plenty of unemployment. Public opinion attributed the distress to various causes: monopoly of the clothing trade by the Merchant Adventurers; excessive carrying out of bullion by the East India Company; overbalancing of imports from the East; usurious exchanges, etc.

The attacks on the Merchant Adventurers concerned Misselden; those of the East India Company concerned Mun. The latter wrote a defence and published it in 1621, under the title *A Discourse on the East India Trade*, in which he pointed out: first, that his Company, when founded in 1601, was licenced by Queen Elizabeth to carry out annually £30,000 in silver bullion and foreign coin (with the proviso, however, that the Company would "import within six months as much gold and silver as shall be equal to the value of the silver exported"),[1] but in the twenty years of its existence it had carried out much less bullion that it was entitled to; second, that the India trade was enriching the country. It bought annually in India drugs, spices, raw silk, and calicoes for £100,000 and sold them partly in England, partly to foreign countries for £494,233. None the less, Mun admits that English trades were depressed, owing to several causes, two of which were abuse of exchanges and non-observance of the statutes of employment (p. 52–53), which all resulted in carrying out of the realm much gold and silver. It is well to remember those two causes, for they are quite old-fashioned and in harmony with the views of Malynes. In 1621, Mun writes simply as an old-time merchant, defending his particular cause. There are no new views, no fireworks in his writings, but sober common sense and mercantile arithmetic.

Mun having defended his Company, Misselden followed suit with a small-sized book (134 pages), entitled *Free Trade* (1622),[2] defending the Merchant Adventurers from the charge of monopolizing the cloth trade, and showing the causes of the depression or—as he writes—the decay of the trade, and proposing remedies. The first edition is not extant in the British Museum, but I infer

[1] The critics of the East India Company stressed the widespread opinion that the Company failed to act up to the proviso.

[2] By "free trade" it was understood in those years the demand for the abrogation of the royal grants of trade monopolies to certain companies, and relaxation of the embargo on the export of money.

from the preface to the second edition that the first edition had given rise to some criticism on account of its being overloaded with Greek and Latin and Hebrew quotations of no direct relevance to the subject. It also caused Malynes to reply with his *Maintenance of Free Trade* (1622), in which he complained that Misselden failed to see the real cause, namely, the dishonest exchanges of the bankers.

In the second edition—so I infer—Misselden inserted (pp. 104–105) an ill-humoured rejoinder to Malynes for his recent agitation in favour of *par pro pari*, which "he has brought to perfection after more than twenty years." Misselden refers evidently to Malynes's *Canker of England*, which appeared in 1601, and must have already seen Malynes's book, *Maintenance of Free Trade*.

The causes of the trade decay Misselden sees in the excess of imports of fineries and luxuries (particularly tobacco); usury; litigation; negligence of the searchers (export inspectors) in allowing inferior cloth to be exported; overvaluation of English and Spanish coin in Holland, so as to force it out of this realm; export of bullion by Turkey, Persia, and the East India Company; the disastrous wounds inflicted by the envious Dutch on the English trade in causing the Indian Princes to embargo the export of the large stock purchased on the India markets by the East India Company, "this great and noble societie," represented by Sir Dudley Digges and that "discreete merchant, Mr. Thomas Mun" (pp. 13–14, 78).

The remedies were: to export more than we import; agreement with Holland to stabilize the rates of the currency; intervention of the King with the Dutch, in order to obtain better treatment for the East India Company and some understanding with them on the East India markets not to outbid one another, and thus prevent the subtle Hindus preying upon Christendom and getting all the bullion out of Europe (pp. 109–113); making bills of debt (domestic bills of exchange) transferable, that is, it should be allowed to give them to third persons in payment for goods or in settlement of debts; fostering the trade with Persia.

Misselden's warm appeal to James I to "revive the languishing body of the East India Company" was of no avail. The following year (1623), occurred in the Dutch settlement of Amboyna the imprisonment of the English traders and the execution of ten of them. The only effect of the appeal was the invitation to Misselden by Digges and Mun to enter the service of their Company.

Meanwhile, something very important must have occurred in the public life of the country, which either gave a new turn to the thoughts of Misselden and Mun or merely precipitated floating ideas into a well-defined doctrine. For we see them jettisoning much of their former views and taking up a new position. The year 1622 formed evidently a caesura in the activities of Misselden and Mun.

Indeed, something very important to the merchant class did come to pass. In 1622, James I and his advisers made two announcements concerning trade and commerce, which signified an unmistakable reversion to mediaeval conceptions:

(i) In May 1622 an order in council was published,

urging upon the "Merchants Committee for enquiry into the decay of merchandise and inequality of trade"—that is, excess of imports—to expedite their report.[1] The King, evidently mistrusting the merchants, appears to have added a large number of members to the committee and turned it into a Commission on Trade, which, as we have learned in a former chapter, consisted of fifty-one members, mostly high state officials and noblemen, who with regard to foreign trade could but advise to bring importations and exportations to "equalitie," that is, to conform to the mediaeval maxim not to buy more than we sell.[2] This advice was, as we know now, of no earthly use to the merchants. They evidently wanted Cato's.

(ii) In June 1622 the King issued a bullion ordinance (Proclamatio contra Exportationem Bullionis), which must have given a shock to the merchants and particularly to those of the East India Company.[2]

Thus the year 1622 added much to the opposition between King and merchants. The first reply of the latter was Misselden's *Circle of Commerce or the Ballance of Trade* (1623). It is in the nature of a mercantile manifesto, but, in view of the great danger of incurring the displeasure of His Majesty, the author assailed with all his cleverness and learning the poor apostle of *par pro pari.* Half of Misselden's tract is directed against the "malignities" of Malynes, and the other half is given to an elucidation and exposition of the essentials and blessings of the balance of trade: "As a paire of scales or balance is an invention to show us the weight of things, whereby

[1] *Calendar of State Papers, Domestic,* 1619–1623, vol. cxxii, p. 384.
[2] Rymer-Sanderson, *Foedera,* vol. xvii, f. 376.

we may discern the heavy from the light and how one thing differs from another in the scale of weight, so is also this balance of trade an excellent and politic invention to show us the difference of weights in the commerce of one kingdom with another . . . If the native commodities exported do weigh down and exceed in value the foreign commodities imported, it is a rule that never failes that then the kingdome grows rich and prospers in estate and stock, because the overplus must needs come in in treasure or merchandise." If the contrary happens, "it is a manifest sign that the trade decays, because the overplus must needs go out in treasure." The main thing, therefore, is "to have the cast of the balance," else the decay of English trades could not be arrested. Besides this illustration and assertion of the balance of trade doctrine, British economics owes to Misselden the term "natural liberty" as inherent in the course of trade.[1]

The Misselden and Mun of the year 1623 and onwards were, as far as trade policies are concerned, quite different from the Misselden and Mun of the years 1621 and 1622. While in point of time it was only a difference of a year or two, the break with the past, though apparently abrupt, was complete and irrevocable.

Misselden learned nothing more, presumably believing that he knew everything there was to be known on earth.

Not so Mun. He made great strides in generalizing his long commercial experience in the Italian centres of trade and manufacture, and reducing it to a doctrine. He grew into the most representative man of the merchants.

[1] Edward Misselden, *Circle of Commerce*, 1623, pp. 117, 123, 131. See *infra*, p. 182, for the full quotation.

It must have been good to consult him and to follow his advice. His views may be summarized as follows:

First, the exportation of money for business purposes, which the legislators and the people think to cause a loss of treasure and consequently the impoverishment of the realm, is in reality increasing the country's treasure.

Secondly, the increase and plenty of treasure *per se* is of no importance, for it but results in an increase of prices. It is, however, of great importance for the power of the state and the welfare and conveniences of the people as a whole.

Thirdly, the balance of trade answers all things in trade and commerce. Neither the royal ordinances nor the trickeries of the bankers, exchangers, and moneyers, neither the stupidities nor the perversities of man, can alter or undo the effects of the balance of trade (*England's Treasure*, ch. 4, 5, 21).

In 1628, the East India Company laid before Parliament a "Petition and Remonstrance," asking for protection for the Company against the Dutch. The ideas embodied in that petition were then elaborated by Mun in his *England's Treasure*, the substance of which is forcefully summarized in the final chapter of his treatise (*England's Treasure*, ch. 21): It is a summing up against royal trade policy, against Malynes and his associates, against all those who accuse the exchangers, the coinage debasers, etc., of ruining the country. It did not ultimately matter whether exchanges moved for or against a country or whether the exchanges were *par pro pari*; even raising or debasing the coinage was of no account. He declares, "Let forraign princes enhance their coins, or debase their standards, and let his Majesty do the like, or keep them constant as they now stand; let forraign coins pass currant here in all payments at higher rates than they are worth at the Mint; let the statutes for employment by strangers stand in force or be repealed; let the meer exchanger do his worst, let princes uppress, lawyers extort, usurers bite, prodigals waste, and lastly let merchants carry out what money they shall have occasion to use in traffiquing. Yet all these actions can work no other effect in the course of trade than is declared in this discourse. For so much treasure will be brought in or carried out of the commonwealth, as the forraign trade doth over or under ballance in value. And this must come to pass by a necessity beyond our resistance."

Mun died in 1641, on the eve of the Civil War, probably in full confidence of the victory of the merchants, who were destined to rule the trade and commerce of the nation. In the same year, Dudley North, the first consistent free-trade economist, was born.

5. *Influence of the Balance of Trade Doctrine*

Thomas Mun's treatise became a text-book of commerce. At that time the opposition to the exportation of bullion and foreign coin (but not of English coin) practically disappeared. In 1663, free exportation of bullion and foreign coin was made lawful. The final trade balance ruled as the main mercantile doctrine.

Even Sir William Petty, a first-rank economic thinker, could not escape the all-pervading influence of the balance of trade doctrine. To the question, how to employ our people? "I answer generally we shall employ ourselves by raising such commodities, as would yield and fetch money from abroad . . . But when should we rest from this great industry? I answer, when we have certainly more money than any of our neighbour states, both in arithmetical and geometrical proportion." In another place he concurs in the view that "the great and ultimate effect of trade is not wealth at large but particularly abundance of silver, gold and jewels, for these are wealth at all times and all places," while other commodities are "riches *hic et nunc*." In another passage he calls gold and silver "universal wealth."[1] But Petty, as we shall show in a later chapter, was already involved in a process of transition to more advanced views.

John Locke, far greater as a moral philosopher than as an economist,[2] was completely under the influence of mercantilist theory. He thought that "upon examination it will be found that our growing rich or poor depends . . . only on which is greater or less, our importations or exportations of consumable commodities . . . The overbalancing of trade, between us and our neighbours, must inevitably carry away our money, and quickly leave us poor and exposed. Gold and silver, though they serve for few, yet they command all the conveniences of life, and therefore in a plenty of them consists riches." He wrote that in 1692, and four years later he confirmed that view, by writing that "by commerce silver is brought in only by an overbalance of trade," that is, "when the

[1] Sir William Petty, *Economic Writings*, ed. Hull, pp. 147, 259–260.

[2] Maybe, a moral philosopher, writing about Locke, would begin by saying: "John Locke far greater, as an economist than as a philosopher."

quantity of commodities which we send to any country do more than pay for the goods we buy from them. For the overplus is brought home in bullion."[1] At the time of Locke, however, the balance of trade doctrine was beginning to be subjected to much criticism. Still, we find also that it had adherents till about 1730. Sir Isaac Newton, writing as Master of the Mint, declared that "the safety and increase of the coyn depends principally on the ballance of trade. If the ballance of trade be against us the money will be melted down and exported to pay debts abroad and carry on trade in spite of laws to the countrary." . . . To obtain "a ballance for us, luxury in foreign commodities should be checkt and the exportation of our commodities encouraged."[2] Jacob Vanderlint, a humanitarian London merchant, in a treatise which would teach how to make money plentiful and the nation happy, writes, "Money (by which understand always gold and silver) can be brought into a nation that hath not mines, by this means only, viz: by such nation's exporting more goods in value than they import. For, in proportion as the value of exports exceeds the value of imports, money, which must balance the account, increaseth . . . And this is called and doth constitute the general balance of the trade of all nations that have not mines."[3] Finally, Cantillon, an Irish-French merchant and economist, declares: "It is this balance of trade which enriches nations in the present situation of the world, as the acquisition of bullion, of which money is made, is that

[1] John Locke, *Works*, 1723, vol. v, pp. 12–13, 148.

[2] W. A. Shaw, *Select Documents*, ed. 1935, p. 138.

[3] Jacob Vanderlint, *Money Answers All Things* (1734), ed. Hollander, pp. 12–13.

which acquires to one nation, comparing with another, its superiority of power, force and influence."[1]

The supreme importance attached to foreign trade had, as explained above, its counterpart in the disregard of the home market. This is one of the outstanding characteristics of mercantilism. Mun held that the exchanges in the home market were unprofitable, "for the gain of one subject is the loss of another." Only in exchange with foreigners was there profit "and the Commonwealth gains" (*England's Treasure*, ch. 14). Petty assumed that the wealth of every nation consisted chiefly in its share which they have in the foreign trade with the world, rather than in the domestic trade. This opinion is shared by John Hales, Charles Davenant,[2] the author of *Britannia Languens* (pp. 289–290), John Pollexfen[3]—all writers of authority and some of them in high official positions. Home trade was merely a circulation of goods, that is, valuable things, from one person to another, without increasing the treasure of the Kingdom. The wealth and poverty of kingdoms depended solely on the balance of trade, on the relation between exports and imports.

[1] Richard Cantillon, *Analysis of Trade*, London, 1759, p. 33.

[2] Charles Davenant, *Works*, vol. i, p. 163.

[3] John Pollexfen, *Discourse of Trade*, p. 40, 154; *Id.*, *England and East India Trade*, 1697, p. 20.

IX

IMPORTANCE OF MANUFACTURE

1. *Arts and Crafts as Sources of Treasure*

Till about the year 1570, English overseas trade consisted mainly in the exportation of native raw materials as well as of undressed cloth, and in the importation of manufactured goods, luxuries, etc. This was the material basis of the age-long royal customs and bullionist policy. In the opinion of the merchants, however, trading of that nature was impoverishing the country, for it resulted in overbalancing import values.

The question, then, to which the balance of trade doctrine gave rise, was this. If an excess of exports over imports was absolutely necessary to prevent the outflow of gold and silver and thus to save England from impoverishment, what were then the most profitable commodities to export in order to bring home the highest balance of treasure?

The answer was not slow in coming. Not to send out raw native commodities, that is, wool, woolfells, unwrought and undyed cloth, in which the materials contain more value than the labour spent on them, but to send commodities in which the value added by skilled labour exceeds by far the value of the materials, that means manufactured goods, or, as they called it in the sixteenth century, "artificialtes," that is, wrought by artificers or craftsmen. Armstrong, writing about the year 1535, declares, "Surely the commonweale of Englande muste rise out of workes of the common people. The workes of husbandry encreseth plentie of vitalles and the workes of artificialte encreseth plente of money."[1]

Crowley, in his epigrams, sums up the advantages of manufacture:

> "This realm has three commodities,
> Wool, tin, and lead,
> Which being wrought in this realm,
> Each man might get his bread."

Hales divides the trades or "misteries" into the three classes, according to their effect on decreasing, consuming, and increasing treasure in the realm. "Some, like mercers, haberdashers, etc., doe fetche out our treasure of the country," and therefore are not necessary to the commonwealth. To the second class belong shoemakers, tailors, carpenters, etc., who get their living in the country, "but bring in no treasure unto us." Therefore, we must cherish well the third class, "and these be cloathiers, tannars, cappers, worstedmakers, glovers, papermakers, sylver and goldsmiths . . . nedlemakers, spinners and some others . . . Such occupations alone doe enrich divers countries that be else barren of themselves."[2]

We find the same idea a century and a half later in a treatise of John Pollexfen, Commissioner of Trade and Plantations, who declares, "A great difference shall be made between such trades and imployments that in their nature and design tend to get and bring riches into the

[1] *T.E.D.*, iii, p. 127.
[2] John Hales, *A Discourse*, pp. 91–92, 64.

nation, and those that can only serve to make it change hands."[1]

Manufacture was so closely connected with the acquisition of treasure that Hales asked, what need was there to travel to Peru for gold and silver, when of common clay, of various plants and woods of little value as raw materials, costly commodities could be made and were being made by foreign workmen and sold for gold and silver in English markets? Couldn't Englishmen do the same?[2]

The same question was asked and answered by London merchants: they brought over skilled Flemish weavers, German miners, Dutch papermakers, and befriended many religious refugees who had special skill in their arts and misteries, to teach the English workpeople craftsmanship, to create new trades, in order to promote the export of "artificial wares."

The terms "artificialtes" and "artificial wares" were later superseded by the term "manufacture," which is most probably of Italian origin, since Italian towns were the earliest in Christian Europe where arts and crafts flourished. Ludovico Guicciardini, in his famous description of the Low Countries (1567), and particularly of the international commerce in Antwerp, employs the term *manifattura* several times and defines it as "consisting of the industry and work of man." In the French edition, which appeared in the same year, it is translated as "manufacture et qui consiste en l'industrie et travail de l'homme." There is no English translation, but an abridged paraphrase of the book was published in 1593,

[1] John Pollexfen, *England and East India*, 1697, p. 7.
[2] John Hales, *A Discourse*, p. 64.

where *manifattura* is paraphrased as "made with hand of artificers."[1] In English mercantilist literature we find the term "manufacture" from 1622 onwards, it came into general use probably through Francis Bacon, who employs it often in his works.[2] "There can be but three things," he writes, "which one nation selleth into another; the commodity as nature yielded it; the manufacture; and the vecture or carriage." But it is much more profitable to sell manufactured goods to the foreigner, since "the increase of any estate must be upon the foreigner" and to ship them in our bottoms so as to get the cost of freight and insurance too. "And it cometh many times to pass . . . that the work and carriage is more worth than the material and enricheth a state more" (*Essays*, XV). This was accepted and acted upon in foreign trade. The object aimed at was to export as little as possible of natural commodities, but much workmanship and freight, for these constituted the greatest values and enriched a country most. These views are expressed in a lucid way by Mun (ch. 3, 12):

"In all things we must endeavour to make the most we can of our own, whether it be natural or artificial," but the main stress is to be laid on the export of artificial commodities. "We know that our own natural wares doe not yield us so much profit as our industry. For iron ore in the mines is of no great worth, when it is compared with the advantage it yields . . . being cast into ordnance, muskets and many other instruments of war for offence

[1] L. Guicciardini, *Descrittione di Paesi Bassi*, Anversa, 1567, folio 124; *Description of the Low Countries*, London, 1593, p. 38.

[2] Francis Bacon, *Works*, ed. Spedding, Ellis, Heath, vol. iv, p. 269; vol. vi, pp. 410, 448, 588.

and defence, wrought into anchors, bolts, spikes, nayles and the like for the use of ships, houses, carts, coaches, ploughs, and other instruments of tillage. Compare our fleece-wools with our cloth, which requires shearing, washing, carding, spinning, weaving, fulling, drying, dressing and other trimmings, and we shall find these arts more profitable than the natural wealth."

Mun uses often the terms "industry" and "manufacture"; in our days the term "industry" has displaced the term "manufacture," but its meaning is clear. By "industry" we understand the production of those commodities in which the value added by workmanship exceeds by far the value of their materials.

2. *Beginning of the Protective System*

In the sixteenth century, when Flemish and French commodities were superior to the English, the furtherance of manufactures in England required protective duties. Such a policy was advocated as far back as in the first half of the sixteenth century. The author, either Armstrong or another, of a treatise written about 1530, pleads in his ardent way for fostering "artificialte" by all means, even if at first the price of the goods be higher than the foreign ones: "Better it were to pay six pennies for any thing made in the reame than to pay four pennies for a thyng made out of the reame, for those six pennies is owres to spend in the reame and the four pennies spent owt of the reame is lost and not ours. If a right order of a common weale may be said in England to have vittals as plentifull as in old tyme, artificialte to be meynteynyd shall cause as good chepe artificialte as in other reames and muche more substantiall."[1]

Hales pleads for an identical policy. "It weare better for us," he argues, "to pay more to owre owne people for those (artificial) wares than lesse to the strangers; for how little gaines so ever goeth over, it is lost to us cleare. But how much so ever the gaines be that goe from one of us to another, it is all saved within the Realme." In order to carry out such a policy he would have the import of such commodities either stopped "or els burdened with such a custom that, by the time it come hither, our men might afford" their goods "better cheape than strangers might doe theirs, the custome considered."[2]

In the reign of Elizabeth, in which the mercantile interests controlled trade legislation, the protective system was systematically applied, and under its fostering care the various branches of manufacturing and English shipping gradually developed, and grew in the course of the seventeenth century into one of the most important factors of English economic life. It was the strength of manufacture and traffic that enabled the mercantile classes to fight down to the bitter end all royalist and aristocratic obstacles that stood in the way of the commercial ascent of England, and to lay the foundation of the British Empire. In 1663, Samuel Fortrey, a fairly progressive and influential economic writer, could declare, "On them (that is, manufacturers) chiefly depends both the wealth and prosperity of this kingdom."[3] And there is an instructive description of manufacturing progress in John

[1] *T.E.D.*, iii, p. 105. [2] John Hales, *A Discourse*, pp. 64–66.

[3] Samuel Fortrey, *England Interest*, ed. Hollander, p. 23.

Cary's *An Essay on Trade* (1695): "The refiners of sugar lately sold for six pence per pound what yielded twenty years since twelve pence; the distillers sell their spirit for one third part of what they formerly did; glass-bottles, silk-stockings and other manufactures (too many to be here enumerated) are sold for half the prices they were a few years since, without falling the labour of the poor." And all this was done by the ingenuity of the manufacturer and the improvement he made in his working methods. Thus stockings were woven instead of knitted, "tobacco is cut by engines instead of knives . . . deal boards are sawn with a mill instead of men's labour; lead is smelted in windfurnesses instead of blowing with bellows." Every day new projects were being set on foot to render woollen manufactures easier.[1]

By "manufacturer" is meant the craftsman. This was, as a rule, still the meaning of the term at the beginning of the nineteenth century. As soon, however, as the craftsman left his own domestic workshop and his own tools and entered, with bare hands, as a wage worker into the factory, the owner of the factory took the name of manufacturer.

3. *Sir William Petty on Money, Value, and International Trade*

In economic reasonings of ancient, mediaeval, and modern times it was uniformly assumed that value consisted in utility, that is, in the capacity of a thing to satisfy human wants. From the time of Aristotle onwards, moral

[1] John Cary, *An Essay upon Trade*, pp. 145–147.

philosophers, schoolmen, economic writers, taught that want (*indigentia* or *necessitas* in the language of the schoolmen) caused men to associate with one another, for singly they were unable to satisfy their wants.

Want made society.

The wants of men are similar—all men want shelter, food and clothing. But division of labour made men dissimilar in their abilities to satisfy those wants—some men were builders, others shoemakers, tailors, tillers of the soil. The dissimilarity of occupations made men exchange their goods against one another.

Exchange turned men into an association for mutual service.

But in what proportion should those associates perform their mutual exchanges? Natural justice demanded that exchange should be equitable—utility for utility, value for value. Here a difficult problem arose. Were all wants of men of equal degree of urgency, equality of exchanges would offer no difficulties. Since, however, the wants differ in degree, how should the goods, which were destined to satisfy them, equitably exchange against one another? It is no reply to say that the order or degrees or the classification of wants should be the order, or degrees, or classification of the values of the goods. This reply merely shifts the question from the particular to the general. The question as to the equalization of the various orders or degrees of wants and goods remained open.

Aristotle (*Politics*, I, ch. 3, pp. 13–16, and *Ethics*, V, ch. 5) and the schoolmen, who wrote commentaries on them, replied that for the purpose of exchange and equalization of the goods money was invented. But money, as they taught us, was a measure and not a valuer: money merely indicates the valuations set upon the goods by their producers or traders or buyers.

St. Thomas Aquinas, in his commentary on Aristotle's *Ethics* (book V) interpreting the philosopher, remarked that equality of exchanges meant also equality "in labore et in expensis," both goods should be equal as to labour and cost spent on them. None the less, he came finally to the conclusion—or rather gave way to the authoritative view of Aristotle—that want (or utility) was the real measure of value.[1] Strictly speaking, then, it is not money that measures value; it only indicates the value that utility sets upon things.

Some schoolmen, as also John Hales and Erasmus, added rarity (scarcity) to utility as one of the essentials of value, which was undoubtedly a step forward in the researches about value; still, with all that there was no objective measure for making exchanges equal and prices just.

In practice, therefore, all reasonings about equality of exchanges and *iustum pretium* found their expression in statutory prices, customary market prices, and—with the growth of commerce—in the "law" of supply and demand.

The growth of manufacture in the last decades of the seventeenth century could not fail to influence and stimulate economic thought. The view that wealth and prosperity of the Kingdom depended on manufacture

[1] "Hoc autem unum, quod omnia mensurat, secundum rei veritatem est indigentia" (St. Thomas Aquinas, *Comment. in Ethic., Aristot.*, liber v, lectio 9, sub b.c.f.).

began gradually to dominate economic policy. Merchants, manufacturers, and scientists worked hand in hand to improve production. Economic thought ceased to be centred on the sphere of circulation, that is, on commerce and traffic, and was moving to the sphere of production for export. Not the market but the manufactory became the centre of economic speculation.

New questions and ideas arose as to the meaning of wealth and its source, as well as to the factors that determined the value of the produced goods. In the sphere of circulation, in commercial transactions, it was universally acknowledged that plenty and scarcity made things cheap or dear. There was no objective measure of value but the empirical. Or, as the old maxim expressed it, "Valet quantum vendi potest," a thing is worth what it can fetch. The higgling of the market fixed the price. But how were we to ascertain the value of the merchandise that were going to leave the manufactory for a potential market? What was their natural value?

The first English economist who was preoccupied with those questions was Sir William Petty. He is the pioneer of the English economics of production. He stands in the middle, between the past great mercantilist writers—John Hales, Misselden, and Mun—and the coming great industrial economists—Adam Smith and the Ricardians. His mind worked in the transition period between mercantilism and industrialism. Petty enunciated new truths and relapsed into old views; he often repeated himself and often contradicted himself. The productiveness of his intellect far outran the speed of his pen; his English was by no means of classical purity or correctness.

None the less, he must be regarded as the initiator of English classical economics: he laid the foundations on which his successors—Smith and Ricardo—could erect their structure.

Petty's leading principle is that labour, skilfully and economically applied, is the source and measure of value of agricultural and industrial commodities, including money. Labour is the active principle of wealth-creation. Of his books it is the *Treatise of Taxes*, published in 1662, *Quantulumcunque* (1682), and *Verbum Sapienti*, published posthumously in 1692, which contain his ideas on value and money. "If a man," he writes, "can bring to London an ounce of silver out of the earth of Peru in the same time that he can produce a bushel of corn, then one is the natural price of the other; now if by reason of new and more easie mines a man can get two ounces of silver as easily as he formerly did one, then corn will be as cheap at ten shillings as it was before at five shillings, *ceteris paribus*."

Labour, in the sense of Petty, is not limited to wage labour. It does not mean that the wageworkers are the creators of value. He thinks of labour as embracing the whole process of production, getting raw materials, planning, managing, and procuring the upkeep of all who labour in the process of production. Petty declares: "Suppose a man could with his own hands plant a certain scope of land with corn, that is, could dig, or plough, harrow, weed, carry home, thresh and winnow so much as the husbandry of this land requires and had withal seed wherewith to sowe the same, I say that when this man hath deduced expense and what he hath himself eaten;

the remainder is the true rent. How much English money will this corn or rent be worth? I answer so much as the money, which another single man can save, within the same time, over and above his expense, if he imployed himself wholly to produce and make it: viz. let another man go travel into a country where is silver, dig it, refine it, bring it to the same place where the other man planted the corn; coyne it, etc., the same person all the while his working for silver, gathering his food for his necessary livelihood, procuring himself covering, etc.; I say the silver of the one must be esteemed of equal value with the corn of the other."

Here we have the real equation between commodity and money. The equal amount of labour bestowed on the production of commodity and on a number of grains of silver makes them commensurable.

The superiority of the industrial economist over the mercantilist is best seen in the conception of international trade. Petty expresses the opinion that the profit in international trade arises from the difference in the aptitude of certain lands for the production of certain commodities. The gain of one is not the loss of another, but one country gains because it can produce a certain commodity with less labour than the other. Such a country has, as it were, "a natural monopoly," and can sell dear and buy cheap. A country will prosper if it can produce commodities with the least labour. And this can be done by higher skill, division of labour, that is, dividing the productive process of a commodity into several operations, each of which being assigned to a single workman, and "facilitation by art," by which Petty, as a member of the Royal Society, meant better tools and the application of mechanical contrivances.

The standard of value as given above might have appeared quite satisfactory, but Petty, in his pioneering way, searching for the most exact standard, expressed also the opinion that land and labour were the two denominations of value, that is, we ought to say that a certain manufactured commodity was "worth so much land and labour." It is not quite certain what he meant. He had, however, in this respect two successors, Richard Cantillon and Joseph Harris, economic writers who likewise regarded land and labour as the true standard of value, and who attempted to elucidate its meaning. Their conclusion is that value consists in (i) rent of land, labour, and expenses incurred by the farmer or mine-owner in the production of the raw materials; and (ii) labour and expenses bestowed by the manufacturer on transforming the raw material into a commodity. In the final analysis, "the value of labour is to be reckoned the chief standard that regulates the value of commodities."[1]

Petty deals with rent in connection with interest on money. It has with him two meanings: first, rent is the net produce, or the surplus of corn that remains to the farmer after having deducted all expenses, labour cost, and the cost of his own sustenance. Secondly, the part of

[1] R. Cantillon, *Analysis of Trade*, pp. 21–22, 1759; J. Harris, *Of Money and Coin*, 1755, ed. McCulloch, pp. 350–352; Adam Smith, who generally regards labour as the standard of value, looks also to the price of corn as the standard. I believe that these difficulties arose from the fact that in the seventeenth and eighteenth centuries rent payments were very often made in a certain number of bushels of corn, and not in money, so that a quantity of corn, the product of land and labour, was regarded as a unit of the value of land.

the net produce paid by the farmer to the landowner, according to supply and demand, quite in the same way as the borrower pays interest to the creditor. The demand for land increases with the growth of population. The same factor is the cause of the rise of the price of corn, and consequently of the rise of rent of land. Petty touched also on what became later known as differential profit and differential rent, which may accrue to the farmer or landowner owing to the advantage of situation. "As, for example, if the corn which feedeth London, or an army, is brought forty miles thither, and there is corn growing within a mile of London, or the quarters of an army, then this corn shall have added to its natural price so much as the charge of bringing it thirty-nine miles doth amount unto."

As mentioned in a former chapter, Petty could not escape the influence of the mercantilists with regard to treasure and balance of trade doctrine. But, as an economist engaged in a transition to liberal views, he also declared that "the keeping or lessening of money is not of that consequence as many guess it to be of." He was for free exportation of money, also for an abatement of protective customs duties on all commodities "not fully wrought and manufactured, such as raw hides, wool, raw-silk, cotton, as also tools and materials for manufacture." His transition to a moderate liberalism proceeded, as everywhere in those times, on the basis of the conception of natural laws and natural liberty. He regarded the usury laws "as against the laws of nature." It was vain and fruitless to make civil laws where nature was concerned. In all matters concerning "Politicks and Oeconomicks it is best to act as those wise physicians, who tamper not excessively with their patients, rather observing and complying with the motions of nature than contradicting them by violent administrations of their own."[1]

Petty appears here as a budding Whig, with all the virtues of Whiggism: political shrewdness joined to advanced economic views. He also shared the failings of the Whigs, which will be dealt with in a later chapter.

4. *Petty and his Contemporaries on Labour, Population, and Wages*

The economic writers contemporary with Petty shared the opinion as to the wealth-creation quality of manufacturing labour. A few of them are worth quoting. Sir William Temple declares epigramatically, "The time of labouring or industrious men is the greatest native commodity of any country."[2] The author of *Britannia Languens* writes that "by manufacture a nation will be made rich and powerful. Most materials of manufacture are of little value whilst raw or unwrought, but by manufacture they may be made five, ten or twenty times their first value, according to workmanship." The author complains that our youth are reading too much Homer and Vergil, and Hebrew authors, and too much of science, but nothing of

[1] Sir William Petty, *Economic Writings*, ed. Hull, 1899, pp. 42–48, 50–51, 55–56, 60, 118–119, 192–193, 259–260, 446. Hull's opinion that Petty owed his labour value theory to Hobbes has hardly any foundation. All that Hobbes says in English and Latin about commodities and their value is that "God gives His goods either freely or sells them for labour to mankind" (*Leviathan*, ch. 24; *De Civitate*, ch. 24). This "theory" Petty could have learned right enough from the Bible (Gen. 1, 29–30; 3, 19).

[2] Sir William Temple, *Works* (1672), ed. 1814, vol. i, p. 129.

trade, and they are so puffed up with learning that they call the artificers "mechanick fellows." Yet, the clergy, the liberal professions, and the shopkeepers, do not increase our wealth. It is only the "labours of the people, bestowed in this way (i.e. in manufacture), which glomerate the riches of the world and make any nation a prodigy of wealth; for while vast numbers of manufacturers are thus continually improving the value of some commodity or other, they work for the nation . . . as well as for themselves; if 100,000 manufacturers get £6 per annum apiece, the nation must gain or save £600,000 per annum by their labour, supposing the materials be meliorated only to the value of their wages."[1]

Locke argues, "It is labour indeed that puts the difference of value on everything. If we rightly estimate things as they come to our use, and cast up several expenses about them, what in them is purely owing to nature, and what to labour, we shall find that in most of them ninety-nine hundreth are wholly to be put in account of labour."[2] Sir Walter Harris writes, "In the white clothes, all that we make of them above the cost of wool and oil is raised upon the labour of our people and is clear profit to the Kingdom. Suppose the wool and oil for one piece of cloth cost three pounds and that the cloth yields thirteen pounds, the ten pounds is raised by the labour or workmanship of the manufacturer."[3]

The valuation of the labour of the people in terms of riches led to the view that an increase of population

[1] *Britannia Languens* (1680), pp. 298, 301, 357, 478, in McCulloch's *Select Tracts*, 1856.

[2] John Locke, *Of Government*, II, §§ 40–42.

[3] Walter Harris, *Remarks on England and Ireland* (1691), p. 129.

was a blessing to the country and ought to be encouraged, for, as Petty said, "Fewness of people is real poverty."[1] This opinion was quite general. It was thought that England was under-populated, and many complained of the drain of the population caused by emigration to the colonies (plantations). "People are in truth the chiefest, most fundamental and precious commodity out of which may be derived all sorts of manufactures" (*Britannia Languens*, pp. 350, 358). Sir Josiah Child declared that the riches and poverty of any civilized country was proportionate to the plenty and paucity of its population, but, at the same time, he formulated the following theory of population: "Such as our employment is for the people, so many will our people be: and if we should imagine we have in England employment but for hundred people and we have born and bred hundred and fifty people, I say the fifty must go away or starve" (*New Discourse*, ch. 10). The two opinions, which he expressed in the form of axioms, are apparently contradictory, but Child really meant that the plenty and paucity of population, and, consequently, the riches and poverty of any civilized country, ultimately depended on the enterprising merchant, who created the opportunities for the labouring population to produce wealth and to increase their own number by procuring them employment. Capital, then, controlled the movement of population by giving or withholding employment, that is, the means of subsistence.

From the fact that labour was extolled as the source of wealth it must not be inferred that the mercantilists were

[1] William Petty, *Economic Writings*, 1899, p. 34.

a sort of Labour Socialists. Their attitude towards the labouring people was, as it will be shown on the next page, anything but friendly. With the exception of Thomas Mun and those economic writers who propagated mercantilist views in the years before the Civil War, nearly all the later mercantilists were antagonistic to the working classes. Their appreciation of labour was, and was meant to be, a glorification of the Third Estate. The later mercantilists were guided by the view that the property and wealth of the Third Estate had their legitimate source and moral justification in the personal endeavours of the merchants and tradesmen, in contradistinction to the property and wealth of the landed nobility, whom they thought to have come to their lands by violence or royal favouritism. This appears to me to be particularly the real sense of Locke's conception of labour and property.[1]

The same may be said of the paradoxical phenomenon that the rise of the English and French middle-classes, the real representatives of individual property, was theoretically supported by appeals to primitive communism of jus naturale. Locke, in his famous treatise, *Of Government*, one of the most influential books of its time, and the French writers after him, always start from the premise that originally the earth was common. This argument, however, was by no means intended to propagate communism, but was meant to defeat the claim of the nobility that the land belonged to the lords. The moral philosophers argued against the feudal maxim, "Nulle terre sans seigneur," and maintained that originally

[1] John Locke, *Of Government*. II, §§ 27, 40-42.

the land was common and belonged to all the people, but was violently appropriated by the nobility.

The attitude of the later mercantilists, beginning with Petty, and the attitude of the merchants in general to the workpeople was illogical, but practical. In the abstract the craftsman was a being endowed with labour power, the active principle of wealth, and with manufacturing skill capable of enriching the country. In practice, he was thought to be one of the mass of the labouring poor—improvident, lazy, with a propensity to drunkenness and debauchery. As soon as he had enough to eat he would refuse to work. It was, therefore, necessary to keep the working people poor and needy, in order to stimulate the incentive to build houses and roads, to spin and weave, dye cloth, knit stockings, tan hides, dig coals, smelt iron ore, cast ordnance, etc. It was an old, sad ditty on the English workman. In the last quarter of the sixteenth century, William Harrison, writing on the changes of his day and particularly on the rise of the Tudor country houses, described them as so "magnificent and statelie" that they often matched the palaces of princes. And they were built by English workmen who "are in a manner comparable in skill with old Vitruvius, Leo Baptista, and Serlo. Neverthelesse, their estimation more than their greed and covetousness . . . caused them to be rejected and strangers preferred . . . who are more reasonable in their taking and lesse wasters of time by a great deal than our owne."[1]

This is a very mild rebuke, and is accompanied by a flattering recognition of the skill of the English workmen.

[1] *T.E.D.*, iii, p. 68.

The mercantilist writers of the century prior to the Civil War, that is, when the middle-class was still struggling for power, were, as already mentioned, friendly to the workpeople. Thomas Mun, in particular, never failed to plead in favour of the workman. He asked the masters, who owned and enjoyed the fruits produced by the craftsmen, to care for the well-being of the workpeople.[1] He even expected that the taxes on bread should be compensated by a corresponding rise of wages, so that the burden should fall on the rich, "who are either idle, or at least work not in this kind, yet have the use and are great consumers of the poor's labour . . . And if they (i.e. the rich) should peradventure fail and therefore to abate their sinful excesses and idle retainers" it would be a gain for the Commonwealth. (Mun, *England's Treasure*, ch. 3 and 16). By "rich," Mun understood the nobility.

After the victory of the middle-class, the mercantilist writers, with few exceptions, turned against the working-class. It began with Petty. "It is observed by clothiers and others, who employ great numbers of poor people, that when corn is plentiful, the labour of the poor is proportionately dear, and scarce to be had at all, so licentious are they who labour only to eat, or rather to drink." Therefore, a certain part of the corn, when the harvest is good, should be stored "rather than the same should be abused by the vile and brutish part of mankind." Such a storage would prevent the overfeeding of the people and

[1] Thomas Mun writes, "For as much as the people which live by arts are far more in number than they who are masters of the fruits, we ought the more carefully to maintain those endeavours of the multitude in whom doth consist the greatest strength and riches both of King and Kingdom" (*England's Treasure*, ch. 3, § 12).

so indisposing them to their usual labour.[1] Petty, himself the son of a poor clothier, but endowed, like Francis Bacon, with preternaturally rich gifts of intellect, and borne along by material and social success, forgot his humble origin.

John Houghton, who, like Petty, was a Fellow of the Royal Society, writing about the same time as the latter, relates as a fact—and the Royal Society dealt only with facts that could be numbered, weighed, and measured—that it "is common with the weavers to be drunk on Monday, to have the headache on Tuesday, and their tools out of order on Wednesday." Likewise, the silk-stockingers, who "had a great price for their work," seldom worked on Mondays and Tuesdays, but spent most of their time in ale-houses or at nine-pins."[2] Sir Josiah Child, the banker and Governor of the East India Company, gave his weighty opinion that when victuals were cheap "the poor in England will not work above two days in a week, their humour being such that they will not provide for a hard time, but just work so much and no more as may maintain them in that mean condition to which they have been accustomed,"[3] but to his honour it must be said that he was against low wages.

These views concerning the working people, commonly called the "poor" or the "labouring poor," were held by the great majority of the well-to-do. Only a few reformers, such as John Bellers and Vanderlint, looked upon the poor with the eyes of humanitarians.

[1] William Petty, *Economic Writings*, pp. 274–275.
[2] John Houghton, *Collection of Letters* (1681), p. 177.
[3] Sir Josiah Child, *New Discourse of Trade* (1693), p. 18.

The conclusions from such views were inescapable. The poor should be kept poor, lest they cease producing wealth and enriching the country. Wages should be low and victuals dear, so that the poor could not withdraw themselves from labour.[1] From Defoe and Mandeville to Arthur Young, that is, throughout the first three quarters of the eighteenth century, those views were propagated in season and out of season, and Arthur Young summed them up in a sentence: "Every one but an idiot knows that the lower classes must be kept poor or they will never be industrious."[2] Moreover, not only should they be kept on short rations, but be managed, controlled, and disciplined by the masters, "who"—as Thomas Mun said—"enjoy the fruits of labour."

It was this class, shrewd and hard in business and foreign affairs, yet liberal and tolerant in politics, religion, and human thought, that laid the foundation of modern England and her industrial and parliamentary system.

In a century and a half—from 1500 to 1650—they rose to political power. "The Commons were weak at the accession of the Tudor dynasty, they were comparatively poor and accustomed to be ill-treated by the aristocracy, and they were unversed in public affairs. The Tudor sovereigns had taken chosen members of the middle-class into their immediate confidence and had administered the local affairs of the country by them and with them. Then had come the influx of wealth by commerce and manufacture, and the spirit of adventure by which that wealth

[1] See E. S. Furniss, *Position of the Labourer*, 1920, who deals extensively with these questions.

[2] Arthur Young, *Eastern Tour*, 1771, iv, p. 361.

was directed to our shores. The Commons had grown independent in prosperity by the hardihood with which they struggled for pre-eminence in social life. In 1485, they were but a down-trodden portion of the English people, looking out for a strong ruler to defend their cause. In 1603, they were almost identical with the nation itself, with aims and ideas of their own, and with firmness and resolution enough to strengthen them to carry out the thoughts that their hearts conceived."[1]

5. *Conflict between Crown and Merchants*

With the growth of the trading classes, the leading mercantilists were getting quite emphatic in their assertion that not customs, subsidies, and impositions, but traffic and the manufacture of commodities were the most appropriate and effective means to bring money into the country and consequently into the exchequer. To quote the best known mercantilist authority: "The main thing," wrote Thomas Mun, about the year 1630, "is to possess goods; if you have them you will get money. He that hath ware hath money by the year. . . . The only way to force treasure into the country and to make it stay in the country is by balance of trade."[2] In the course of time the royal monetary policy and the merchants' commodity policy came into collision with one another.

In Hales's *A Discourse* (1549) one of the disputants (the doctor) argues: "While strangers may afford wares made by them better cheape than wee may the same make here,

[1] Gardiner and Mullinger, *Introduction to the Study of English History*, ed. 1894, pp. 127–128.

[2] Thomas Mun, *England's Treasure* (chs. 4, 21).

and yet that it were better for us to bye our owne thoughe thei were deerer." The doctor was pleading for the fostering of native production, particularly of manufacture, whereupon the other disputant, the knight, rejoins: "Marie, theare you speake a thinge that the Kinges attornie would not agree unto; for if such ware weare made within the Realme, then the Kinges custome should be lesse, by reason that litle or no such wares should come from beyond the sease."[1] The same opposition of interests between royal revenue and promotion of native manufacture is clearly expressed in *The Pleasaunt Poesye of Princelie Practise*, written in 1548 by William Forrest, who pleaded for a restriction of wool export in order to give English weavers, fullers, etc., an opportunity for making cloth.[2]

In the reigns of Henry VIII and Elizabeth the merchants had pretty well their way. The conflict between the two policies was therefore dormant, but it grew all the more acute with the accession of the Stuarts, who in their trade legislation looked back to the Angevin models.

The exponents of the ideas of the merchants were, as we have shown, Misselden and Mun, while Milles and Malynes wrote for the Stuarts.

Misselden in a clever pamphlet formulated the conflicting views in the following manner. "The matter of trade is either natural or artificial. The natural matter of commerce is merchandise, which merchants from the end of trade have stiled commodities. The artificial matter of

[1] John Hales, *A Discourse*, pp. 65–66.

[2] *England in the Reign of Henry VIII* (Early English Text Society), 1878, p. xcvi.

commerce is money which has obtained the title of sinews of war and of State." But the proper rank of things was perverted and like "old Jacob who blessing his grandchildren crossed his hands and laid his right hand on the younger and the left on the older. And money, though it be in nature and time after merchandise, yet forasmuch as it is now in use became the chiefe."[1] This remarkable utterance I interpret as a disguised attack on the paternal bullionist policy of the kings who, like the Hebrew patriarch, favoured the younger before the older offspring. For he deprecated the bullionist laws and he was the first writer to introduce into British economics the term "natural liberty" as inherent in the course of commercial life. "Trade has in it," he writes, "such a kind of natural liberty in the course and use thereof, as it will not endure to be fors't by any."[2] Misselden was terrorized into dissimulation by the King's "Proclamatio contra Contumelias," issued December 20, 1620.[3] One must read that dictatorial proclamation against the utterance of any adverse view on royal policy and one must also recall to mind the imprisonment of Pym in 1621, as well as the persecution of Chief Justice Coke in 1622, in order to understand why, for instance, Thomas Mun preferred

[1] Edward Misselden, *Free Trade*, London, 1622, p. 7. It is worthy of notice that his opponent, Gerard Malynes, who was the spokesman of the Stuarts, replied in the same year that "money, being the right judge and rule which giveth or imposeth a price unto commodities, is the thing *active*, and commodities become *passive*" (*Maintenance of Free Trade*, London, 1622, p. 15).

[2] Edward Misselden, *Circle of Trade*, 1623, p. 112. The author of that passage was so terrified that, while saying that law of nature is of universal validity, he adds that God and the King are above the law of nature!

[3] Rymer-Sanderson, *Foedera*, vol. xvii, folio 275.

not to publish *England's Treasure* in his lifetime. And Misselden was by no means as courageous as Mun. Only on the very eve of the Civil War could the London merchant, Lewes Roberts, tell Charles I some mercantilist home truths: "It is not our conquests, but our commerce, it is not our swords, but our sails that first spread the English name in Barbary, Turkey, Armenia, Muscovy, Arabia, Persia, India, China and indeed over and about the world; it is traffic of our merchants and the boundless desire of that nation to eternize the English honour and name that has induced them to sail and seek into all corners of the earth." Roberts demanded the establishment of a Board of Trade, staffed by merchants, to direct the foreign trade.[1]

To render the opposition of views and interests as manifest as possible we draw here a clear line of demarcation between the two doctrines and policies. Common to both—to bullion ordinances and balance of trade doctrine—was the idea that treasure was the aim of foreign trading and the most effective embodiment of wealth. But while the Crown regarded customs, subsidies, etc., as the source of treasure (coin and bullion), which, if once brought to the Treasury, should be kept at its disposal and should no more be allowed to leave the country, the merchants looked upon money in the first instance as a means to successful trading, and the increase of treasure as the final effect of the balance of trade, provided the money could be as freely handled by the merchants as any other commodity. In the first period the King and his customs revenue (in coin and bullion) formed the centre of all

[1] Lewes Roberts, *Treasure of Traffike*, 1641, p. 52.

trade policies. In the second period the merchant and his commerce and manufactures gradually moved to the centre of public life. The merchants argued that "when the subjects have, the King has," provided he obtains the consent of the Commons. The subjects came first and then the King.[1] The two views ultimately clashed. It was, in the last analysis, a question as to who should control money and foreign trading—the Crown or the merchant class.

Royal bullion policy and merchant balance of trade, money and commodity, the Crown and the mercantile classes, came into collision with one another. The two vital functions of society, production and defence—defence in the broader meaning of State action in peace and war—and production in the broader meaning of the whole economic life—could not be harmonized.

The juxtaposition of two opinions about the merchants, expressed by two leading contemporaries in books dedicated to their respective sons—namely by King James I in *Basilikon Doron* and by Thomas Mun in *England's Treasure*—illustrate in a striking manner the irreconcilable opposition between the Stuarts and the Third Estate in the four decades before the Civil War.

The semi-mediaeval King James I tells his son that "the merchants thinke the whole common-weale ordained for making them up; and accounting it their lawful gaine

[1] Thomas Mun, writing about the year 1630, declares that the people "are never pleased except their contributions are granted by general consent. For which purpose the invention of Parliaments is an excellent policie of government . . . There could nothing be devised with more judgment for the common quiet of a Kingdom, or with greater care for the safety of a King" (*England's Treasure*, ch. 17).

and trade to enrich themselves upon the losse of all the rest of the people; they transport from us things necessarie, bringing backe sometimes unnecessary things and at other times nothing at all. They buy for us the worst wares and sell them at the dearest prices; and albeit the victuals fall or rise of their prices, according to the abondance or skanteness thereof, yet the prices of their wares ever rise, but never fall; being as constant in their evill custome, as if it were settled Law for them. They are also the speciall cause of the corruption of the coyne, transporting all our coyne and bringing in forraine, upon what price they please to set on it."[1]

With these views the Stuarts tried to govern a country in which the foremost spokesman of the merchants tells his son that the merchant is "the steward of the Kingdom's stock," that his trading is a "noble vocation" and ends his book with the following panegyric on the merchant:

"Behold then the true form and worth of foreign trade, which is the great revenue of the King, the honour of the kingdom, the noble profession of the merchant, the school of our arts, the supply of our wants, the employment of our poor, the improvement of our lands, the nursery of our marines, the walls of our Kingdom, the means of our treasure, the sinews of our wars, the terror of our enemies" (*England's Treasure*, ch. 21).

Mun speaks here as Abbé Siéyès will speak one hundred and fifty years later in France. What is the Third Estate economically? Everything! And what is the Third Estate politically? Nothing! The contradiction must be resolved

[1] James I, *Basilikon Doron*, in *Works* of James I, Cambridge, Mass., 1918, p. 26.

if England is to live. The mercantilist writings in the hundred years between 1540 and 1640 are much more than economic treatises about money and the balance of trade. They are one long campaign for the political control of trade and commerce by the merchant class, that is, for a new balance of state power.

X

RECAPITULATION

1. *The Meaning of the Balance of Trade*

Among the material forces that led the European man from mediaeval to modern times, money (coin and bullion), known as treasure, stood pre-eminent. The monarchy needed it in order to be able to fuse the loose collection of feudal manors and trading cities into a centralized state. Customs duties in their various forms levied on imports and exports were the principal source of the Crown's bullion income. Trade and commerce, the agencies of imports and exports, were looked upon by personal monarchy mainly as a means to obtain treasure and to keep it at the disposal of the Crown. Money was the sinews of state. The valuation of money was the prerogative of the Crown.

The rise of the middle-class, that is, the trading and mercantile class, began towards the end of the fifteenth century, when the state was fairly centralized and the old aristocracy had been either killed or subdued. The middle-class, like the monarchy, depended on money. The aims of both were at first identical—getting treasure and subduing the feudal order, "the insolent nobility," as Thomas Mun used to say. The Crown needed money for political ends, the merchants needed money for economic purposes. Trade could never have outgrown the primitive stage of barter but for the invention and constant increase of money. It was money that quickened the growth of trade and moved and carried the commodities into the stream of circulation. The rise of the English middle-class happened to synchronize with a stringency of money, caused by a considerable expansion of Western trading, without a corresponding expansion in the supply of precious metals. The monetary resources of civilized Europe proved inadequate and were but slowly supplemented by Mexican and Peruvian silver, which the Spanish conquistadors were bringing to Europe since the third decade of the sixteenth century, but much did not reach the English shores before 1560. Meanwhile, the need for money was acutely felt. The merchants looked upon money in the first instance as a means to increase trade, which, in its turn, would increase treasure, provided it was allowed freely to operate. "Money begets trade and trade increases money," wrote Thomas Mun, and it could not do so by fiscal regulations and prohibitions, but by the balance of trade, that is, by an excess of exports over imports, for it was an unfailing rule that the balance must be paid in coin or bullion. The achievement of such a balance was the proper business of the merchants and within their competence. It could never be achieved by the state.

"Balance of trade" became in those times a formula—a vague formula, for none of the mercantilist writers who spread this doctrine could demonstrate how it could be applied. Still, there was a meaning in it, as there generally is in all formulas, of an economic, political, or social nature. Such formulas are but flags that cover the goods, and it is the business of the historian or statesman to discover them. The balance of trade formula covered economic and political essentials. England, having no gold and silver mines of her own, could only obtain bullion by a flourishing foreign trade in manufactured goods. And nothing but large balances of exports could give the merchant class coin and bullion, that is, liquid assets, and enable it to develop manufacture and establish trading companies for oversea traffic, for, while nature and the craftsman's skill and ingenuity are the sources of all wealth, it is traffic that converts it into treasure.[1] The liquid assets had to be in form of bullion, since credit and banking were still in their swaddling-clothes. The contest for the balance of trade was a struggle for liquid assets.

Crown and merchant class became ultimately competitors, they competed for the selfsame object—treasure, but by different methods, which resolved themselves into the question, pregnant with fate, as to who should control trade and commerce: the Crown or the merchant class? The Civil War decided in favour of the merchants, and they took charge of the economic life of the nation.

The balance of trade formula had also another meaning. It was the expression of the opposition of the rising commercial classes to the still lingering doctrines of mediaeval ethics. The principle of commutative justice demanded equality of exchanges, *par pro pari*, with a

[1] The earth and "artificial commodities," writes Lewes Roberts, "are the true sources of wealth. Two things are necessary for the production of artificial commodities or manufactures, (i) workmen or arts masters, who yield an abundance of things wrought; (ii) their efficiency, skill, ability, which gives true credit to the fabrics and works. But even the earth and labour wouldn't enrich a country without traffic" (Lewes Roberts, *Treasure of Traffike*, 1641, p. 9, in MacCulloch's *Early Economic Tracts*).

certain allowance for gain, which, according to the teaching of the schoolmen, should be sufficient for sustenance, as a salary or wage for the labour of the merchant. Men, and particularly Christian men, living together in society, were—and originally intended to be—associates for mutual help. Human wants brought them together for the mutual exchange of their works and services, and thus to constitute a peaceful and harmonious community.

With those principles of natural law and Christian ethics no accumulation of liquid assets was feasible. Equality of exchanges brought no gains to be converted into assets. And yet they were indispensable. For, how else could we drive trade, develop manufacture, produce commodities for exports, in order to force treasure out of the neighbouring and distant countries and to enrich our own country? And we were in need of riches, not only for traffic, but for the strength and safety of our commonwealth. "For that which produceth riches, doth consequently beget strength and safety, so farre forth as treasure is accounted the principal nerve and sinews of war, either offensive or defensive."[1] Another mercantilist writer declares, "Treasures are those vehicles that carry out men of daring spirit, mighty thoughts and abilities, into the conquest of forraign countries."[2]

The new trading interests, borne along by emotions of national patriotism, came into collision with Christian ethical doctrine. In this conflict the balance of trade formula was the battle-cry of militant mercantilism.

Once we have grasped the meaning of the balance of

[1] Lewes Roberts, *Treasure of Traffike*, p. 111.
[2] *Britannia Languens*, 1680, p. 187.

trade as the most effective means in those times to acquire liquid capital for the purpose of developing manufacture or increasing national power, we have got the solution of all those contradictory statements and confusions of thought with which the mercantilist writers are generally charged.[1] The main indictment against the mercantilist was drawn up by Adam Smith. In *Wealth of Nations* (book IV, ch. 1) we read as follows: "I thought it necessary, though at the hazard of being tedious, to examine at full length this popular notion that wealth consists in money or in gold and silver . . . Some of the best English writers upon commerce set out with observing that the wealth of a country consists, not in its gold and silver only, but in its lands, houses, and consumable goods of all kinds. In the course of their reasonings, however, the lands, houses, and consumable goods seem to slip out of their memory; and the strain of their argument frequently supposes that all wealth consists in gold and silver, and that to multiply those metals is the great object of national industry and commerce."

The indictment is well founded. To refer only to Misselden and Mun, it is beyond doubt that they regarded commodities as wealth and trade as their aim. Yet both of them were pioneers of the balance of trade, the main purpose of which was to make the country rich through bringing in treasure, the universal embodiment of wealth, as Petty called it. But as soon as we look upon the mercantilist conception of treasure as meaning liquid capital, all contradictions disappear. No doubt, lands, houses, etc., were wealth, but no trade and commerce could be driven

[1] E. Lipson, *Age of Mercantilism*, iii, p. 62 *passim*.

by them. In view of the backwardness of credit and banking, houses and lands could not be converted into liquid assets, and without these no commercial transaction was possible. Bills of exchange were a costly makeshift, which finally had to be honoured with money.

After the establishment of the Bank of England, the increase of paper money, the growth of credit and banking since the end of the seventeenth century, the conditions that gave rise to the balance of trade doctrine gradually disappeared. To a rationalist like Adam Smith, to whom the world appeared as a wonderful mechanism, with secret springs and wheels, and whose conception of history necessarily lacked the organic view of development, the mercantilist doctrine and policy was nothing else but an absurdity and one of the follies of which past history consisted.

2. *Mercantilism and Foreign Politics*

The opposition of interests between merchant class and Crown, the conflict between new trading practice and mediaeval ethics, were not the only antagonistic elements that lurked in mercantilism. The balance of trade formula was the flag that covered vast expansionist ambitions. It was the economic expression of a vehement dynamic drive outwards. This policy as practised by the merchants was the economic basis of nationalist and imperial politics. The nationalist consciousness of the merchant class set itself in hostile opposition to all foreign countries which, by their prosperity and rising balance of trade and power, threatened the English balance of trade and power. Sir

William Petty and John Locke, the most famous political and economic writers of the second half of the seventeenth century, declare, "that a nation is only rich when it is richer than its neighbours." Petty's opinion on this matter was quoted in a former chapter. Locke says, "riches do not consist in having more gold and silver, but in having more in proportion than the rest of the world, or than our neighbours."[1] The maxim that trading with foreign countries can be advantageous only if the latter are made to lose treasure, or that the profit of one nation is the loss of another, must needs lead to hostility among the nations, and ultimately to war.

It was Francis Bacon who stated the warlike policy of the mercantilist period. In dealing with neighbours, he writes, the unfailing rule is "that princes do keep due sentinel that none of their neighbours do overgrow so, that by increase of territory, by embracing of trade . . . become more able to annoy them than they were. And this is generally the work of standing counsels to foresee and hinder it." Bacon combats the view of the schoolmen "that a war cannot be justly made but upon a precedent injury or provocation. For there is no question but a just fear of an imminent danger, though there be no blow given, is a lawful cause of a war" (*Essays*, XV).

None of the leading mercantilist writers is free from jealousy and hostility against prosperous neighbours. Mun devotes a long chapter (19) to the demonstration that the Dutch "do undermine, hurt, and eclipse us daily in our navigation and trades," and therefore should not be allowed to fish in "his Majesty's seas," and if the Dutch

[1] John Locke, *Works*, ed. 1723, vol. v, p. 13.

thought they were entitled to fishing, "I will only say that such titles would be sooner decided by swords than by words." Fortrey's *England's Interest* is partly an attack on France, whose manufactures were taking out of England balances of several hundred thousand pounds.

It was in those times an easy matter to scare the nation by drawing up an adverse balance of trade, since nobody could really disprove it. And as soon as it was felt that England was getting overbalanced in wealth by the Dutch or the French, war was near. Even the enmity between England and Spain in the last quarter of the sixteenth century, for all dynastic and religious differences, arose mainly from the feeling that Spain by her enormous wealth—the sinews of war and state—drawn from Mexico and Peru, was by her overbalance of power threatening the existence of England.

All the wars fought in England since the last quarter of the sixteenth century up to Waterloo—wars against Spain, the Dutch, the French—were caused by mercantilist considerations and motives, that is, balance of trade and its political counterpart—balance of power.

It was an astonishingly strong class of men who, in the course of three centuries, settled accounts with Papacy and personal monarchy, as well as with all their commercial and maritime adversaries, built up manufactures and reared a vast, world-wide Empire. Merchants and adventurous sailors accomplished all these feats. There were no Hamlets among them. Only Shakespeare was the Hamlet: he but saw the ghastly decay of the last Angevins, and the tragi-comic degeneration of mediaeval knighthood. He discerned nothing of the new forces that were building the British Empire. There is no trace in his dramas of a Gresham or Mun, of a Hawkins or Drake. His dramas mirror an England that was out of joint and dying, and not an England that was constructing and renewing her strength.

Two positive qualities and one negative quality appear to be requisite for bringing great imperial and social policies to fruition. The two positive qualities are—first, a few sound guiding principles—the crystallization of the fermenting and floating necessities of a class or a nation; secondly, strong, resourceful, and single-minded leaders. The negative quality consists in the absence of dreams about vast crusades and missions, which are supposed to have been handed down by the past, or entrusted by destiny, to the new generation. Unlike the mediaeval Germans, who were haunted by the dream of being the successors to imperial Rome, and unlike the Russians, who for two centuries pursued the *idée fixe* of being the heirs to the Byzantine Empire, the English pioneers of the mercantilist period simply followed their day-to-day interests, breaking down obstacles, weathering storms, and marching ahead with their balance of trade flag unfurled. They had no vast designs, but minded their own business. Their treatises, mainly written by merchants, are briefs for or against certain demands, regulations, and laws, or they contain practical rules for carrying on trade. There was only one theorist—Francis Bacon. He widened the balance of trade into the balance of imperial power. What Macchiavelli signifies for building up a national state, Bacon signifies for rearing an empire.

XI

TRANSITION TO LIBERAL ECONOMICS

1. *Introductory Remarks*

In the last forty years of the seventeenth century, the public interest was in a growing measure concentrating on economic discussions. This applies particularly to the decade 1690–1701—a decade teeming with thought on all trade activities of the nation. The subjects discussed were: the rate of interest most favourable to trade, and should it be fixed by Act of Parliament or allowed to find its "natural" level?; the overbalancing growth of French manufactures and commerce under Colbert's system of state control and protective duties; import prohibitions of certain French wares; financing of the war with France; the trading activities of the East India Company and their influence on home manufactures; doubts about the validity of the balance of trade doctrine; credit and banking; deterioration of the coin through clipping and the necessity of recoinage (1695–1696); various demands for free commercial intercourse; thoughts on natural liberty and self-acting economic laws.

A far greater number of economic tracts were published in those years than ever before in a similar length of time. The most important authors—important on account of their originality and influence on contemporary or later thoughts—were: William Petty, Dudley North, and the unknown author of the *Considerations on the East India*

Trade. They brought new views and undermined old views. Next in importance were: Samuel Fortrey, on fostering of manufacture and for free export of bullion; Josiah Child, the head of the East India Company, adversely criticizing the mercantilist balance of trade; the anonymous author of *Britannia Languens*, the compendium of all mercantilist views; John Locke, the eclectic of mediaeval and mercantilist doctrines on interest and money; Charles Davenant, a copious writer in defence of free trade for the East India Company; John and Henry Pollexfen, firm advocates of mercantilism and home manufactures as against the East India Company's imports of calicoes, muslins, etc., and export of bullion; Nicholas Barbon, who elaborated and amplified Child's arguments against the validity of the balance of trade as a criterion of the economic state of the country; Roger Coke, in his *England's Improvement* (1675), the only readable one of his tracts, pleaded for a more liberal commercial policy; John Cary and Walter Harris, merchants and manufacturers, staunch defenders of home manufactures. This enumeration does not exhaust the list of the writers of that remarkable period in the history of English economics.

All of them, except Petty, Sir Dudley North, and Locke, wrote with a conscious bias to defend or combat certain group or party interests, and they used as instruments the economic thoughts and formulae created in the past, either for or against those interests. But such biased and partial reasonings and polemics are well-nigh inevitable in economics and politics. Given a diversity of interests in society a divergence of views necessarily follows and must be made allowance for by the economic and political enquirer; his only business would appear to be to find out which of those views are right, but this cannot be arrived at by ratiocination, since the major premise is in each case supplied by interests; he can only endeavour to discover which of the views, notwithstanding their class origin, are in consonance with the general interests or the general trend of social development. The task of the historian—in contrast to that of the politician—is here easy enough, for it is history herself which sifted and tested the truth of either. The following instance may serve as an illustration:

Sir Josiah Child and Sir Charles Davenant—so books tell us—argued against the balance of trade as a criterion of the economic state of the Kingdom, while Pollexfen appealed to that doctrine as the true rule of trade. In fact, however, their references to that doctrine were arguments in a very practical struggle for or against the East India Company. The trade depression at the end of the seventeenth century was ascribed by Pollexfen, Cary, and others to the export of treasure to the East Indies and the excessive imports of calicoes, muslins, and silks, which competed with the English staple trade of woollens. The depression meant the impoverishment of the Kingdom—that is, according to the balance of trade doctrine—diminution of treasure, overbalance of imports. Child and Davenant endeavoured to demonstrate that the balance of trade was not a valid rule of trade nor money the main wealth, and the export of treasure, far from impoverishing the nation, enriched it. They had to re-examine that doctrine and the whole economic position of the Kingdom.

But who was right?

The legislators answered: Pollexfen and his friends, and they harassed the East India Company with restrictions and prohibitions, and, in 1700, it appeared that the career of the Company was going to be altogether cut short.

History answered: Child and Davenant. The eighteenth century is one long demonstration that the East India Company's exports of treasure and imports of Indian textiles did not impede the development of the English textiles nor the growth of wealth. The East India traffic brought riches, and ultimately made England master of India herself. How absurd appeared, then, the balance of trade doctrine! And it so appeared to David Hume and Adam Smith.

To return to our general view of the period, we may state that by eliminating the non-essential and temporary problems, such as the rate of interest, recoinage, the controversy about the attitude towards France, we see the following factors at work for new economic views:

(i) The continued growth of manufacturing, despite intermittent checks; (ii) the development of credit and banking and the introduction of paper money; (iii) the demands for greater freedom of trade; (iv) the spread of the ideas of natural liberty and laws of nature working in matter and mind, in man and his activities, for the happiness and perfection of mankind.

2. *Manufacture, Credit, Banking, and Free Trade*

The second half of the seventeenth century is with regard to economics a parallel to the second half of the fifteenth century. In the latter period, that is, early modern times, it was the relatively rapid growth of foreign commerce that dominated economic thought and gave birth to the doctrine of the balance of trade, which superseded the mediaeval principle of equality of exchanges. In the second half of the seventeenth century, it was the growing importance of the production of marketable commodities in manufacture and agriculture which began to dominate economic thought and government policy. Mercantilism gradually gave up the search for treasure, and concentrated on developing the productive forces at home; it became a system of protection. And in oversea lands it looked not for treasure-trove, but for colonies with raw materials for home production.

In the same measure as this system was doing its work, that is, opening up all the springs of production, it became partly obnoxious by its excesses (prohibitions and prohibitive tariffs, which reacted unfavourably on exports) and partly superfluous and, therefore, an encumbrance. The effect was the rise of free-trade tendencies—first, against prohibitions and excesses of protection, and then against the system as a whole, thus superseding mercantilism in all its expressions, and restoring, if only in theory, the principle of equality of exchanges.

The title of Thomas Mun's main treatise and the first sentence of Adam Smith's main work illustrate the change in economic thought. Mun treats of treasure won in commerce by overbalances, upon the foreigner; Smith treats of the wealth to be won for all by labour in factory, mine, and field, and to be exchanged to the equal benefit of all nations.

Next in importance was the development of credit, banking, and paper money. In the last decades of the seventeenth century a great part of home trading was carried on by means of credit. The goldsmiths were the bankers, who accepted deposits of money and issued notes, which passed current in trade. In 1694, the Bank of England was founded and, three years later, it began to issue paper money (bank notes). In 1698, domestic bills of debts were invested with legal sanction and could be assigned by the holders to third persons in payment of debts.[1]

Money was divested of its gold and silver glamour, turned into a commodity, and made, as Davenant says, "a servant of trade," much like the divestment of monarchy of its exalted position and making it a servant of the nation (1689).

The conception of money as a mere commodity was being henceforth more and more accepted by economic writers, so that the die-hard mercantilist, Joshua Gee, writing in 1729, broke into the lament that people were indifferently looking on how the "money, the only true token of treasure and riches," was being carried away; "but they say that money is a commodity like other things and think themselves never the poorer for what the nation daily exports."[2]

The class of people who engaged in credit and banking became known as the "moneyed interests," and they were very active. Daniel Defoe, well versed also in

[1] Cf. E. Lipson, *Economic History*, iii, p. 220 *passim*.

[2] Joshua Gee, *The Trade and Navigation of Great Britain*, ed. 1730, p. 8. The tract went through five editions.

commerce, writing in 1692–1693, relates that "about the year 1682 began the art and mystery of projecting to creep into the world. First came military invention, then shipping, projects at penny post, stock jobbing became general."[1]

On the basis of credit and banking the "local wealth," as Petty called the real and movable properties and possessions (lands, houses, shops, magazines, workshops, furniture, etc.), could be converted into "universal wealth," that is, into coin. The facilities thus offered to traders for obtaining liquid capital broadened the concept of wealth till it comprehended all sorts of values, thus undermining the balance of trade doctrine, and making room for free-trade movements.

At the beginning they were only directed, as mentioned before, against import prohibitions and prohibitive tariffs, but not against protection as such. Protective duties were, as a rule, regarded as necessary and wholesome; yet the idea of international traffic, and the whole political atmosphere, created by the authors of the Glorious Revolution, attracted writers who were either in sympathy with those commercial interests which needed more freedom, or purely with the idea of natural liberty, the legacy of the Civil War and which Filmer (*Patriarcha*, p. 4) regarded as "a vast engine of popular sedition." And as it often happens with intellectual stimuli, when they once get logic into working order, the mind appears to grow into a sovereign creator and produces thoughts and theories of which the initiators never dreamed or of the implications and consequences of which the writers themselves are

[1] Daniel Defoe, *Essay on Projects*, ed. 1887, pp. 32, 42.

hardly conscious. So it was in this case with such writers as Davenant and particularly with Sir Dudley North and the anonymous author of the *Considerations on the East India Trade.*

3. *The Anti-mercantilists: Child, Barbon, Davenant*

The anti-mercantilists, in endeavouring to undermine the balance of trade doctrine, had to argue against its two main propositions and their corollaries. First, the proposition that treasure is universal wealth which makes the nation rich and the state powerful. Second, that the balance of trade is the guiding rule for getting treasure. The corollary of the first proposition is that export of treasure impoverishes the country and is, therefore, to be prohibited. The corollary of the second proposition is restriction of imports by high protective, or even prohibitive duties, and encouragement of exports.

The anti-mercantilists, therefore, endeavoured to demonstrate that wealth consists in all things that satisfy human wants, that is, wealth consists in commodities, and that treasure is a commodity like any other. Secondly, that an embargo upon treasure is a prohibition of the export of a commodity, and that all prohibitions of either exports or imports are injurious to the country. In arguing against the second proposition and its corollary, the anti-mercantilists moved towards a free-trade policy.

Sir Josiah Child, from his commercial experience and from his interest in the defence of the East India Company, re-examined the balance of trade as the rule of treasure. He was as influential in the Restoration and post-

Restoration period as Thomas Mun was in the first Stuart period. And according to the more advanced stage of manufacture and commerce he was more advanced than Mun. Child admits that Mun's doctrine was very ingenious for its time and useful for commerce, but it became difficult to employ it now in practice. The quantities given in the custom-house books cannot be taken as a measure of trade and traffic. Some of the most valuable commodities of import and export, such as laces, ribbons, silks, jewels, are, by reason of their small bulk, carried in and out by stealth; even commodities of larger bulk escape the customers. And, as to values, the rates of the customs cannot form the basis of computation of the volume of the foreign trade. Of our own exports some commodities are rated very low, others high—all according to the policy of promoting or impeding the export of some commodities.

The custom-house books cannot, of course, register the proceeds of the sales of our exports, for a good many accidental factors, some unfavourable and others favourable, intervene between the payment of duties at our ports and the sale of the goods in the foreign market. The custom-house does not take account of losses at sea, bad markets, confiscations, bankruptcy of buyers. Goods sent out and rated low may at their arrival in foreign lands advance in price, and if we buy foreign goods for those proceeds the whole transaction will appear according to the custom-house books as a loss to us.

Apart from all those deviations in values and quantities, which make the balance of trade a very uncertain rule, the doctrine itself is unsound. There are countries with an overbalance of exports and yet they are not gainers and continue poor, such as Ireland, Virginia, Barbados. Their exports go largely to absentee landlords and stockholders.

Then there are countries to which we export little and from which we import much. According to that doctrine those countries are enriched and we impoverished. Yet the commodities we receive from them are the materials for our manufactures, our munitions, and trading stock, and we are enriched and made strong thereby. Riches do not consist in money only. "Riches and stock are the same."[1]

The best criterion of the economic position of a country is, according to Child, its shipping. If this is increasing it is safe to say that its trade grows and the nation thrives.

Nicholas Barbon, a London medical man and writer on economic subjects, amplified the arguments of Child against the balance of trade doctrine, and gave them by his reasonings a keener edge. While Child ascribed to that doctrine a certain merit for the conditions of the past, Barbon denied it any such merit. Nations could not regulate their trade by that rule, since it was not discoverable in the custom-house, and even if it were discoverable it would be of no use. For it is not with money that nations drive their trade, but, above all, by exchanging their native commodities. If they improve and increase them the nations prosper. Mun's major premise was that if a person has an annual income of £1,000 and a stock of money of £2,000, and assuming that he spends

[1] Sir Josiah Child, *New Discourse on Trade* (there were several editions between 1690 and 1696), ed. 1695, pp. 153–171.

annually £1,500, that is, an overbalance of £500 against him, he will be poor after four years' time. And if he spends only £500 annually, he will be richer by £2,000. This "simile," says Barbon, "is lame," as the Latin proverb has it: "Similitudo non currit quatuor pedibus." For the stock of a nation is not, primarily, money, but its staple commodities, which can never be exhausted, provided they are cared for and increased by industry and arts. It is the surplus of those commodities that are carried out of the country and exchanged for something that's useful and which our country could not produce. The question as to the kind of commodities to be exchanged for our surplus cannot be solved by the balance of trade doctrine. The only way to know what trade is profitable is by examining not the custom-house books, but which sort of goods would employ most hands in manufactures and shipping.

Assuming the balance of trade is a truth, it does not follow that a balance must be paid in money; it can be paid indirectly in wares. The merchant who imports goods from Flanders can pay the balance with the proceeds of his sales to Spaniards or Italians. "There is but one infallible symptom to know when trading nations thrive and grow rich. That is, when the inhabitants grow more populous, when they enlarge and new-build their cities and towns, and when they increase their ships and naval strength."[1]

An examination of the arguments of Mun and Barbon reveals two different points of view. Mun looks upon the world mainly with the eyes of a merchant dealing in

[1] Nicholas Barbon, *Discourse on Coining*, 1696, pp. 35–52.

merchandise, and endeavouring to get capital to drive trade. Barbon's economic world is formed by the manufactory, the field, and the mineral mines, where commodities, that is, the many forms of wealth, are produced. Mun looks upon the increase of money as the result of the general balance of merchandising between nations; Barbon looks upon the increase of all sorts of commodities as the result of the growth of industry and arts, and attaches little importance to money, since by means of credit and banking any commodity can, in case of necessity, be converted into money. The difference between them was caused by the rapid growth of the importance of manufacture and credit in the second half of the seventeenth century. It is the difference between the first decades and the last decades of the seventeenth century.

Charles Davenant, arguing, though not always with consistency, against the mercantilist conception of riches, gives his own view of wealth: "We esteem that to be treasure, which for the use of man has been converted from gold and silver into buildings and improvements of the country; as also other things convertible into those metals, as the fruits of the earth, manufactures, or foreign commodities, and stock of shipping."

In dealing with the balance of trade, Davenant refers to Child's arguments concerning that doctrine. Davenant stands to Child as Misselden stood to Mun. Child and Mun, both of them leading merchants of the East India Company; Davenant and Misselden, the pampleteers and literary advocates of that Company. Starting from Child's opinion that the true state of trade "is very difficult to be come at" from the custom-house books, he declares "that it is utterly impossible exactly to state the balance between the various countries, since all traffic among nations interpenetrates and reacts upon one another. It is an endless and uncertain speculation consciously to arrange or order the knotted and tangled threads of the wide-flung network of foreign trading and home consumption, so as to effect a balance. People complain, for instance, that we lose in the balance with France. The answer is that perhaps our losing to Frenchmen enables them to trade with Italy and Spain, which are the best and most profitable markets for our commodities. "It is hard to trace all the circuits of trade, to find the hidden recesses, to discover its original springs and motion, and to show" the mutual dependence of international trade transactions one upon another. Perhaps it is quite "out of human light" to do so, for "many time the workings of trade are as unaccountable as the operations of nature."

And here we come to the refrain of Davenant in favour of freedom of trade, which is, indeed, the refrain of all free-trade movements: "Trade is in its nature free, finds its own channel and best directs its own course; and all laws to give it rules and direction may serve private ends, but are seldom advantageous to the public."[1]

It would, however, be a mistake to assume that Davenant, Barbon, and Child were for the abrogation of the system of protection. They were but against its excesses, that is, against prohibitions of, or prohibitive tariffs upon, imports. They were only "in principle" for

[1] Charles Davenant, *Works*, ed. 1771, vol. i, pp. 96, 98, 354, 381-382, 386–388; vol. v, pp. 452, 378.

complete free trade. Still, the course was set towards free trade and away from mercantilism.

4. *The Free-Trade Maxims of Dudley North*

Sir Dudley North, nobleman and merchant, was born in 1641, the year in which Thomas Mun left this world. He had as a boy a dislike for classical antiquities, which made him a bad scholar of an old-time schoolmaster, who believed in the stick as the best method to knock the Latin grammar into the head of his pupils. Young Dudley showed early a bent for trade and mechanics and grew into a merchant of the Turkey Company. He successfully represented the Company in Smyrna and Constantinople for many years, acquiring several living languages and a vast fortune. He then served in London as a Commissioner of Customs and Sheriff of the City of London. A Tory in politics, he was, as an economist, an advanced Liberal—the result of his vast experience in international trade.

In 1690, about a year before his death, he published a tract entitled *A Discourse upon Trade.* In the same year (1690), Child and Barbon brought out their tracts under similar titles, and, four years later, Davenant began his career as an author.

North's publication is a slender tract of thirty pages, but weighty in thought, evidently the product of long and clear cogitations on matters of commerce and money. It deals mainly with coinage and interest on money (usury)—two controversial topics of the time, which made also John Locke into a writer on interest, money, and coinage. North, in his introductory remarks, expresses his thoughts on free trade in a few short sentences, which may be called maxims of an independent mind for the guidance of students. The whole tract reads, indeed, like a syllabus for the study of anti-mercantilism. It declares:

"The true source of riches, or as people say, 'plenty of money,' is the labour of man applied to the land and its fruits. With the surplus of the fruits of their labour people begin to trade, mutually exchanging their native commodities for goods which they require. They will naturally try to buy cheap and to sell dear. In this course of trade gold and silver are in no sort different from other commodities; they are bought and sold, imported and exported, with as good a profit as other commodities. Gold and silver as money do not derive their standing and valuation from the laws, but from their fineness, scarcity, and smallness of bulk. Wherever coined money is undervalued it is melted down into bullion and carried to that market, where it can obtain the best price. Debasing the coin is cheating the people, as much as a shopkeeper using false weights and measures. The extrinsic value of the coin should conform to its intrinsic value."

As to interest, it is not in the power of any legislature to prevent high interest. It depends on the demand for stock. North adds, "I will not say anything to the theological argument against interest on money. But this I shall maintain politically that if you take away interest you take away borrowing and lending."

All controversy and noise about the balance of trade have their origin in fancy. One nation cannot get richer if the other nation loses. For in matters of trade "the whole world is but one nation or people, and therein nations (are) as persons." If one nation loses in trade, all lose, "for all is combined together." The same rule applies to foreign and home trade. The opinion that "the home trade signifies nothing to the enriching of a nation and that the increase of wealth comes out of foreign trade" cannot be substantiated, since "both are connected together." Foreign trade cannot subsist without home trade.

Trade, Sir Dudley North evidently thinks, has its own laws. Therefore, all laws made by politicians to fix prices or to force men to deal in any prescribed manner, "may profit certain persons, but the public gains not." To sum up: "Laws restraining trade, foreign or domestic, relating to money or other merchandise, are not the ingredients to make a people rich, abounding in money and stock . . . No people ever yet grew rich by policies, but it is peace, industry, and freedom that bring trade and wealth."

How the author of such a treatise could have been a Tory in politics is an enigma, considering the fact that the landed interests, whose political representatives were the Tories, worked for high duties on corn imports and for bounties on corn exports, and the governments, Whig as well as Tory, granted all they desired.

Professor Ashley draws the attention of economic students to the fact that all four anti-mercantilists—Child, Barbon, Davenant, and North—were Tories and calls their teaching "Tory free trade," but he fails to show the economic reasons for their anti-mercantilism.[1]

The tract of North soon became very rare. It was surely in advance of its time. It is not known whether it

[1] William Ashley, *Surveys*, 1900, p. 268 sqq.

was designedly suppressed or destroyed. In 1822, McCulloch brought out a new edition, and, in 1856, added it to his collection of economic tracts.

5. *The Economics of the Free-Trade Doctrine*

While Dudley North gave only the final results of his cogitations, without revealing the inductive material of his observations, nor the train of reasoning that led up to them, Charles Davenant and the anonymous author of the *Considerations on the East India Trade* (1701) dealt with the main factors of their doctrine. Both of them wrote in defence of the East India Company, which was being severely handled by the Commons, the English woollen interests, and the mercantilist die-hards, and threatened it with extinction.

Davenant sees the basis of his doctrine in the geographical distribution of the climates and produce of the earth, and the specific capacities of the respective labouring people for certain trades. The manifold and diverse products suitable to the various climates and soils, he believes, are "an indication that providence intended they should be helpful to each other, and mutually supply the necessities of one another." Davenant, with this view, says no more than many a mediaeval and early modern writer said long before him on this subject, as shown in a former chapter. But he goes on to deduce from it the main support for his doctrine—namely, that each country or people, using its natural advantages, should produce only those commodities for which providence manifestly destined them. In following up that providential hint, they will produce with least labour, that is, most economically and thus most profitably, considering that the materials that enter into the respective productions are there easily procurable and the capacities of the labouring people most fitted for such work.

So far, so good. But now Davenant turns advocate and tells his countrymen that providence intended them to be growers of wool and manufacturers of cloth, and not weavers of silk and linen. England could never compete with calicoes, muslins, and silk goods. These goods, which fashion prefers to woollens, are apportioned by providence to the East Indies, and, therefore, are produced there cheapest. By allowing their imports freely to enter England, the people will obtain cheaply their fashionable apparel, thus reducing their household expenses.

Davenant admits that this principle, if generalized in commerce, might destroy some home trades, but it can only destroy the uneconomical ones, which are unsuitable to the country. But there is compensation for such contingent losses: by consuming cheap foreign wares, by wearing calicoes instead of woollens, the country will have a larger surplus of its native commodities for export, which enriches the country and, owing to the lower cost of production, will increase its capacity for competition. *Ergo*, the whole agitation against the East India Company is injurious to the economic interests of the nation as a whole.[1]

Davenant owed something to Petty and acknowledged it. The anonymous author of the *Considerations* owed very

[1] Charles Davenant, *Works*, vol. i, pp. 101–110; vol. ii, p. 334; vol. v, p. 378.

much to Petty, but failed to acknowledge his obligation to him, except by saying in his preface that the "author endeavoured, after the manner of the *Political Arithmetic*, to express himself in terms of number, weight, and measure." Only students of economics could gather from those remarks that the author alluded to Petty. He then informs his readers that "the composition of the book has been very hasty . . . wherefore he thinks himself obliged to beg the reader's pardon for his unnecessary repetitions, for his negligencies, for his affectations, and for every other fault but only want of demonstration."

The book is a thin tract of eighty pages, the latter part of which deals with the advantages that English people might derive from a proper organization of the fishing trade; this part stands in no direct connection with the main "demonstrations" of the author in defence of the East India Company. On the whole, it is easier to summarize—by elimination of all repetitions and "affectations" of the author—and to get at the logic of his reasonings, for they are given in a number of consecutive chapters, while Davenant's anti-mercantilist thoughts are scattered in several volumes and must be first strung together to get at their essentials.

The anonymous author does not primarily take account of the geographical distribution of the productive forces, but makes, if only by implication, Petty's theories concerning labour value and "natural" monopoly his guiding principles.

Riches, says the author, that is, "the true and principal riches, whether of private persons or of a nation, are meat, bread, cloths, houses, the necessaries and conveniences of life; bullion and money are the means to obtain those riches." The value of the things which make up riches is measured by the necessary labour time used in their production. Things are of less value when they cost less labour, and conversely, things are dear when their production requires much labour. Whatever the value of those things—high or low—they are always economical when produced with necessary labour time. Profits in trade arise from the exchange of things of less labour for things of more labour. Losses arise in trade from producing things with unnecessary labour time, for they are economically so dear that they become unsaleable when competing with things of the same kind but produced with the necessary labour time. Such trades are uneconomical and are a waste of labour.

This is the logical structure of the unknown author's economics.

And now comes the application: The East India trade consists in buying for bullion things with less labour and selling them in European markets where the same or similar things can only be produced with more labour. In other words: East India goods are bought cheap and sold dear; hence they yield high profits and bring back more bullion than spent on their purchase.

But—it is objected—this East India trade is destroying home trades and causing unemployment. The answer is: Yes, temporarily it destroys trades, but only the uneconomical ones. At first, it causes losses and inconveniences, but the compensation will not be late in coming. Soon it will act as a stimulant to innovations and improvements; it will prove to be the cause of manufacturing progress and the growth of wealth. For, given the desire of man to emulate, to excel and to achieve success in his work, it is safe to assume that the means by which labour time is reduced to its economical minimum will earlier or later come to be applied to home manufactures—namely, better tools, mills, engines, better ordering of the productive processes and division of labour into more minute operations, each of which assigned to a single workman will greatly enhance his skill. All those improvements will raise the home manufactures to their productive maximum. The opportunities for employing labour will also increase and at wages which—to say the least—will be as good as before, and will make our goods cheap and thus raise our competitive power in the markets of the world.

Therefore, the prohibition of the East India trade amounts really to the prohibition of manufacturing progress. You might as well prohibit all arts and crafts and engines which save labour time.[1]

The anti-mercantilist reasonings of Charles Davenant and the anonymous author are the first peak in free-trade economics.

The economic writings of the first three quarters of the eighteenth century are eclectic, containing both mercantilist and free-trade views. A few of them—Vanderlint, Dekker, Massie, and Hume—are dealt with in the following chapter.

[1] *Considerations on the East India Trade*, 1701, in MacCulloch's *Select Tracts*, 1856, pp. 31–45.

6. *Jacob Vanderlint, Matthew Dekker, and Joseph Massie*

Before proceeding to sum up the economic contributions of those three writers, a few lines must be given, if only for the sake of historical sequence, to the struggle between the Whigs and Tories about the proposed commercial treaty with France in 1713–1714. The Whigs, as opponents of the treaty, found their literary mouthpiece in the mercantilist periodical *British Merchant*; the Tories, who favoured the treaty, were represented by the *Mercator*. The most valued contributor to the *British Merchant* was Henry Martin, to whom some writers are inclined to ascribe the authorship of the *Considerations on the East India Trade*; he wrote also on trade matters in Steele's *Spectator*. The leading writer of the *Mercator* was Daniel Defoe. Both periodicals added nothing to the traditional stock of economic thought. They used the formulas of mercantilism and anti-mercantilism respectively as clubs to bludgeon one another.

A treatise of quite a different category was published in 1734 by Jacob Vanderlint, a London timber merchant, who entitled it *Money answers all Things*. The author, without being aware of any contradiction, combines Locke with North, not mechanically, but adding some instructive reasonings of his own. Vanderlint adheres to the view that "money (i.e. gold and silver) became, by the consent of nations, counters for adjusting the value of all things else" (p. 2). Nations with no mines of their own can only obtain gold and silver "by having the balance of trade in their favour." The quantity of money in circulation determines the price of the goods. The larger the quantity of money the higher the price of the goods (p. 4).

So far it is all Locke, whose authority pressed with the weight of a mountain on the minds of the eighteenth century.

But Vanderlint, in his reasonings on the effects of the quantity theory of money, meets with the problem that lurked in that theory as formulated by Locke, but which the latter never dealt with. If the increase of money has for its effect a proportionate increase of prices, what is the use of trying to obtain the balance of trade in our favour? Does that not simply amount to an increase of the number of counters?

The author replies that "plenty of money never fails to make trade flourish" (p. 7), thus increasing the well-being of the country. The nation becomes hereby populous and industrious, the government obtains more revenue and can increase its strength; luxuries become more general. Some writers complain that luxuries weaken the people. Such complaints are unreasonable. Luxuries are not injurious if used within the bounds of the income. The productive capacity of the country, if properly used, demands more consumers. "Luxury will find its proper bounds, which, if any man transgressed in any extraordinary manner, he would be sufficiently whipped with his own rod" (pp. 21–22, 102).

Not so favourable as an increase of money (gold and silver) has been the increase of banking, credit bills, public securities, which are operating as cash, but are not cash. They "enhanced the price of anything amongst us above the rates our real specie would have supported them." They injured our export and contributed much to the depression of our trade. Our goods became too dear for the foreigner and his goods cheap to us and we buy them, so that the balance of trade turns against us (p. 164).

It is no remedy to prohibit their importation by enacting laws against them. "Prohibitions do but cut off much employment from the people" (p. 42), particularly in shipping and manufacture. "All nations of the world should be regarded as one body of tradesmen, exercising their various occupations for the mutual benefit and advantage of each other" (p. 42). Let trade be free. "No inconvenience can arise from an unrestrained trade, but very great advantage." Trade, if free, corrects its own defects. It is something like a self-acting regulator. Suppose that owing to the high price of our goods the balance of trade is against us and that we, none the less, put no restrictions on imports. The foreigner will thus get our money, but as soon as our quantity of money decreases and his increases, the price of our goods will proportionately fall and the price of his goods will rise. The effect will then be that our goods are cheaper and therefore exportable, while his goods lose the market. We thus get our money back and win new markets (pp. 43–44).

The main thing is to manufacture at home all goods we can, and as cheaply as possible. This can be accomplished by extending our agriculture, by diligent tillage of the soil, so as to make the price of victuals low. Thus wages will be lowered, but by no means the subsistence of the labouring people. Cheap food will surely mean lower rents, but the extension of tillage will result in larger rent totals. Only those goods should be imported which, despite all our efforts, we cannot produce, and which other nations produce owing to their particular climate and other natural advantages. Nature has distributed her gifts among the various countries, so that they should have intercourse with one another and help each other with their natural advantages.

For the well-being of the country four things are necessary: (i) diligent tillage of all available land; (ii) working up the native materials into manufactures; (iii) keeping the price of necessaries within the reach of every consumer; (iv) freedom from government interference. "Let the subjects carry on trade in whatever way or means they possibly can. This is the sole rule concerning trade . . . This is infinitely preferable to any governmental encouragements and restraints in favour of trade, which ultimately will always terminate in mischief to trade" (p. 169).

This is in English the physiocratic maxim: *Laisser-faire, laisser-aller, le monde (commercial) va de soi-même.*

Views similar to those of Vanderlint were published by Sir Matthew Dekker, an East India merchant and Member of Parliament, in his tract, *On the Causes of the Decline of Foreign Trade* (1744). He pleaded for the abolition of all prohibitive tariffs, monopolies, privileged trading companies, for "trade cannot and will not be forced." All prohibitions and interference with the course of trade only recoiled on their initiators. He was also for the abolition of all taxation, in the place of which there should be a single-tax levied on the rich.

Joseph Massie, who in the years 1750–1770 published several short treatises on various matters of trade, is the author of a tract entitled *On the governing Causes of the*

Natural Rate of Interest (London, 1750). From the time of the abrogation of the usury laws in the reign of Elizabeth and the fixing of 10 per cent as the legal rate, discussions cropped up concerning the influence of the rate of interest on trade. In 1621, Thomas Culpeper, merchant, published the *Tract on Usurie*, arguing for a legal reduction of the rate of interest, since 10 per cent was usurious. He and other writers, pleading for the same cause, pointed out that the prosperity, that is, the plentifulness of money, of the Low Countries, was due in the main to their low interest rate, while others rejoined that those writers mistook the effect for the cause: not the low rate of interest caused prosperity, but the plentifulness of money caused the low interest rate. Sir Josiah Child supported the demand of Culpeper, while Sir William Petty deprecated all laws to regulate the rate of interest as fruitless and against the laws of nature. "As to money," he writes, "the interest thereof was before at 10 per cent, forty years ago at 8 per cent and now at 6 per cent, no thanks to any laws . . . The natural fall of interest is the effect of the increase of money" (*Pol. Arithmetick*, ch. 4).

It was that discussion which induced John Locke to write his book, *Some Considerations . . . on the lowering of Interest*, in which, arguing on the basis of his quantity theory, he declares, that when there is little money in proportion to the trade of the country, interest is raised. "For in trade everybody calls for money, according as he wants it, and the disproportion is felt," or in simple language, when there are more borrowers than available credit money at the lenders, interest is raised, and *vice versa*.

Massie finds that the answer of Locke is inadequate. In the preface to his tract mentioned above he apologizes profusely for daring to oppose such a great thinker as Locke. He evidently does not much mind Petty, but he is thoroughly awed by the name of Locke; yet Massie really made a serious contribution to the understanding of the movements in the rate of interest. He argues that the interest rate depends on the profit rate earned in trade. The lender, in affording the borrower the opportunity for carrying on his trade, is rightfully entitled to a share in the profits that accrue to the borrower. Generally, about half of the profits was regarded as the natural rate of interest. In the sixteenth and seventeenth centuries, when only the Dutch and the English had a large foreign trade, the profit rate was high. Consequently, the share of the creditor in the profits was high. In the same measure, however, as the number of the competitors grew—the French, the Swedes, the Danes were now likewise engaged in foreign trading—profits were reduced and, naturally, also the rate of interest.[1]

7. *David Hume*

The reader, on taking up Hume's six essays on trade matters, published in 1752,[2] joins, so to speak, the society of an enlightened gentleman of good breeding, wide

[1] J. Massie, *On the Governing Causes Of . . . Interest*, London, 1750, pp. 49–54.—The interdependence of the rate of interest and the rate of profit was well known to Josiah Child (see *New Discourse*, ed. 1804, pp. 47–48).

[2] David Hume, *Philosophical Works*, ed. Green, 1879, vol. iii, second part, to which the references in the text are made.

humanist culture, classical and modern scholarship; his conversational style is polished, but he is interested in trade affairs only in so far as they affect state politics. He has, as it appears, read Thomas Mun, Josiah Child, Dudley North, John Locke, and also Vanderlint and Massie, and he illustrates and embellishes them with quotations from the Greek and Latin writers, adding sometimes a brilliant remark of his own.

Such are the essays of Hume on commerce, arts and refinement (luxury), money, interest, balance of trade, mercantilist jealousy of the trading nations against one another. They are a reproduction of the main ideas of those writers, particularly of Vanderlint and Massie. He is in so far inferior to Vanderlint, as he exalts the merchant above the manufacturer and farmer, quite in the style of Mun. "The merchants," says Hume, "are the most useful race of men in the whole society." Hume's essays may be summarized as follows:

All material goods come from the soil by the exercise of labour, to which man is driven by his passions (or appetites, as North calls them). With the improvement of agriculture some labourers become redundant and they apply themselves to manufactures, and then to arts of refinement (luxuries). The surplus of the fruits of the soil and the products of manufacture are exported to foreign lands in exchange for goods which we want and they produce. The profit of foreign trade is great, for it is carrying out what is superfluous at home and "what bears no price" (Hume means what is very cheap at home) "to foreign nations, whose soil or climate is not favourable to that commodity" (p. 296), and is, therefore, sold at high prices. Foreign trade thus increases the power of the state and the riches and happiness of the people. Arts and refinements are diffused among the multitudes; luxuries become more general, and if not carried to excess are advantageous to the country, for they stimulate industry and make the money circulate among the people.

Foreign trade brings much money, but this is of no consequence within the country, for "it seems a maxim almost self-evident that the prices of everything depend on the proportion between commodities and money, and that any considerable alteration on either has the same effect, either of heightening or lowering the price" (p. 316). None the less, he has some misgivings about the consequences of the quantity theory of money. It made him entertain a doubt "concerning the benefit of banks and paper-credit," for the greater quantity of money is rather inconvenient (p. 311). It seems, however, that plenty of money stimulates industrial activity. "We find that in every kingdom into which money begins to flow in greater abundance than formerly, everything takes a new face; labour and industry gain life; the merchant becomes more enterprising; the manufacturer more diligent; and even the farmer follows his plough with greater alacrity." For, although the effect of the influx of money is a proportionate increase of prices, yet the effect is not immediate. There is an interval between cause and effect. The merchant and manufacturer, that is, the men who are generally the first to acquire some of the new influx of money, can at once expand their business by purchasing the raw materials at the old prices and employ more hands at the current rate of wages, and, when the new goods are on the market, the prices have risen according to the increased quantity of money.

The rise of prices need not worry us. Some people are afraid that high prices will turn the balance of trade against us. The whole balance of trade doctrine has a very doubtful basis. The custom-house books are allowed to be an insufficient ground of reasoning; nor is the rate of exchange a much better criterion. The facts and figures are so uncertain that everybody can manipulate them to prove his own favourable view. All the worry about impoverishing the kingdom by sending away bullion is groundless. Suppose four-fifths of all the money in the kingdom to be annihilated in one night, and the nation reduced, with regard to specie, to the reigns of Harrys and Edwards, what would be the consequence? Prices of labour and commodities would sink in proportion. What nation could then dispute with us in any market? We would then get all the money back. And, if money were too plentiful, we should have to sell dear and lose the market. "Just as water, wherever it communicates, remains always at level, so it is with money and trade, when in free circulation. . . . It is impossible to keep up money, no more than any fluid, beyond its proper level" (pp. 333–334).

It is all more scientifically expressed than Vanderlint ever could. And now we come to see Hume sharing the misgivings of the former about paper money: "There is a method," so Hume continues, "to sink money below the level, that is, the institution of banks, funds, and paper credit. These render paper equivalent to money and make it supply the place of gold and silver, and raises proportionately the price of labour and commodities" (pp. 336–337).

Here Hume, and for this matter also Vanderlint, are in a fix. For both accepted the view of Locke that money has an imaginary—Hume even says "fictitious"—value. If this is so, why should there be any difference between specie and paper-money? Why should the increase of one sort of imaginary value be advantageous and of the other harmful?

But Hume is not abashed or embarrassed. He points to the advantage which the interval between cause and effect may bring even to an increase of paper-money, "but it is dangerous to precipitate matters, at the risk of losing all by the falling of that credit, as may happen upon any violent shock in public affairs" (p. 337). It is, however, interesting to read immediately after that (on page 338) the confession of Hume: "All these questions of trade and commerce are extremely complicated."

Well, on page 316, the quantity theory of money seemed to be "a maxim almost self-evident," and now the consequences are "extremely complicated."

Hume's theory of interest can be given in a few sentences. "The view," he says, "is widespread that low interest is due to plenty of money. This seems not to be in accord with facts. Since the discovery of the precious metals in the West Indies prices have risen about fourfold; and it is probable that gold and silver have multiplied much more, but interest has not fallen much above half. The rate of interest can, therefore, not be dependent on the quantity of precious metals (p. 321). Money having chiefly a fictitious value . . . the greater or less plenty of it is of no consequence if we consider the nation within itself." In reality, high interest arises from three circumstances: great demand for borrowing; little riches to supply that demand; and great profits arising from commerce (p. 322), and *vice versa*. Hume's theory of the movement of the rates of interest combines Petty and Locke with Massie.

Hume was a confirmed free trader, even more pronounced than Dudley North, though he admitted some exceptions to the general rule. Domestic industry lays the foundation of foreign commerce. The numberless prohibitive measures, in obstructing importations, injure also the home trade. There ought to be free communication and exchange among the nations. "The author of the world, by giving them different soils, climates, and geniuses, intended them to assist one another . . . Were our narrow and malignant politics to meet with success, we should reduce all our neighbouring nations to the same state of sloth and ignorance that prevail in Morocco or the coast of Barbary . . . I shall therefore venture to acknowledge that not only as a man, but as a British subject, I pray for the flourishing commerce of Germany, Spain, Italy, and even France itself" (p. 348).

XII

RETROSPECT: BRITISH ECONOMICS IN 1750

The ultimate authority of the laws and regulations that circumscribed the economic activities of the mediaeval merchant, trader, and craftsman, were Scripture and Aristotle. Holy Writ gave the precepts, and their truths were established by the moral philosophy, by the logic and dialectic of Aristotle as interpreted by the schoolmen. The *Summae* and *Sententiae* of the latter were encyclopaedias of theology, politics, and economics, and through them the views of Aristotelian politics and economics influenced many of the British writers, from John Hales to David Hume. There were, however, some exceptions. Among them William Petty deserves special mention, for he was in economics what Francis Bacon was in philosophy—the emancipator from Aristotle.

In the chapter on Alexander of Hales I remarked that Aristotle's theory of money offered great difficulties to our understanding and that I hoped to be more able to elucidate them after I had worked through the economic tracts bequeathed to us by the early British writers. While analysing Petty's thoughts on value and money, it seemed to me that I had come upon the track of the causes that actuated Aristotle in his reasonings upon money and exchange.

Those reasonings, ascending from the simple to the

more complicated, are contained in his *Politics* (I, ch. 3, §§ 6–21) and *Ethics* (V, ch. 3–5). They may be summarized in their essentials as follows:

Society (community, *polis*) is the highest good. The wants of men created it; all things that are capable of satisfying them are utilities—they are real wealth and riches. The things which man cannot acquire by his own labour are obtained by exchanging the surplus of his own things for those which he requires. Such exchanges are in the nature of barter; commodity for commodity, without gain to one and loss to the other. They are natural, that is, rightful. Heads of communities or states (*oekonomikos vel politikos*, as the schoolmen call them) perform such exchanges for the purpose of supplying the needs of their fellow-members.

There are, however, exchanges that have a different purpose. Traders acquire things by means of money, in order to obtain more money; they do not at all produce things, but buy and sell them with the intention of procuring gain. Such exchanges are unnatural and result in a hunt for money-making without limit.

We have in those views the basis of the schoolmen's—and, generally, mediaeval—teaching about trade and commerce and the importance of strengthening the bonds of society, which latter consideration guided them in their interpretations of scriptural and patristic views on commerce. The whole controversy on exchanges in early modern times arose from the conflict between the new trade practice and the Aristotelian reasonings, which coincided with the teaching of the Bible and the Fathers.

We have already referred to exchanges performed on

the basis of money, but we do not know as yet how—according to Aristotle—money came into use.

In dealing with exchanges (*Ethics*, V) Aristotle declares that, strictly speaking, justice demanded equal division. Etymologically and ethically, *dikaion* (justice) derives from *dicha* (to divide), and *dikast* (the judge) had for his duty to see that the division should be equal. In exchanges, however, we cannot divide things equally, we cannot cut them in equal halves, but we must perform them, as the Pythagoreans said, according to the principle of proportionate reciprocity, or equality of requital. If, for instance, a builder, a shoemaker, a farmer, have to exchange their respective goods for one another, we must first know the amount of labour and expenses they had respectively put into their goods. In Aristotle's text there is some uncertainty whether only the value of the goods must be first ascertained by the labour embodied in them or also by the social standing of the producer, so that the same amount of a builder's labour may, by reason of his social position, be more valuable than that of a shoemaker or farmer. At any rate, the respective values and the degrees of their respective capacities to satisfy the wants must be ascertained in order to make them commensurable. They must be equalized. We must know how many shoes or how many measures of corn are equivalent to a house.

For the purpose of equalizing the values and the degree of their utility, money was invented. Aristotle exemplifies this by the following equation: "Let A be a house, B ten minas, C a bed. Now, A is half B; if a house is worth the equivalent of five minas, and the bed C the tenth part of B, it is plain that five beds are equal to a house." But where did the ten minas come from? Aristotle answers: Men made a mutual compact to give and accept some substance, such as iron, gold, and silver, at first merely defined by size and weight, and finally by impressing on it a stamp. This invention turned barter into a money-getting business, and some think that money is riches and wealth, while others are of opinion that money is a non-entity, a mere fancy value as gold and silver, which are of little use in life, since there is no general demand for them as such, and money is worth nothing as soon as it is called in or displaced by some other commodity. Indeed, *nomisma* (money) does not derive from nature, but from *nomos*, law or custom. It was the stamp that gave it value, and as such it serves also as a pledge, as a guarantee, that we shall obtain for it the things when we want them. In serving as a measure for equalizing exchanges money is useful, and its acquired usefulness makes it into a commodity like any other and subject to fluctuations of value, though the value of money is more constant than that of the others.

Two theories of value are running in Aristotle's reasonings: want, demand or use as the real standard, while the labour and social standing of the craftsman are likewise considered, but not adhered to. The substance of money, gold and silver, were of little use, and in their natural state as raw materials had no value. Only after it had been made into money did it receive a value from its usefulness in exchange, so that its value is based on convention and custom. Convention made it and convention can unmake it.

Two questions arise from Aristotle's reasonings. First, how did money as a utility equate the values of the work of the builder and cabinetmaker? (How did B make A and C commensurable?) There is no answer to it in Aristotle's *Ethics* or *Politics*. In practice, the state fixed the prices of the home commodities, and in foreign trade it was demand and supply or custom that determined the price.

The other question is, why should the work of a builder, a shoemaker, or a farmer, have its natural value according to the labour and expenses spent on them, or according to the social standing of the producer, while gold and silver, which have to be dug, refined, turned into bullion, and cut into coin, have no natural value, and become a commodity only through being stamped, that is, by being made into a statutory measure?

I could obtain no answer to that question until I came to Petty's exposition of the labour value theory, which is dealt with in a previous chapter. According to Petty, a pound of silver produced by a man in Peru with a certain amount of labour and cost and overhead expenses, and a certain quantity of corn produced by an Englishman on his land with an equal amount of labour, cost, and overhead expenses, will be of equal natural value. The prime cost of production gives them their natural value and the equal cost of production makes them commensurable.

I then analysed the difference between Aristotle and Petty as regards money and its function. With Aristotle, money has no natural value; it is merely a price-indicator, a counter, by reason of its denomination. With Petty, money has a natural value by reason of the labour and cost bestowed upon it; money is a commodity which, owing to certain of its properties, has become the most desirable commodity; the denomination stamped upon it merely indicates the amout of labour and cost bestowed upon it. With Aristotle, the function of money is to make various quantities of different commodities commensurable by indicating that they all have the same price; it is the sameness of the price that makes them commensurable. With Petty, money and other commodities are commensurable if they all embody an equal amount of labour and cost; money has only this advantage that it shows at a glance how much labour and cost it embodies.

While thus analysing both theories the hypothetical case occurred to me: suppose gold and silver could be dug, refined, etc., without labour and expenses. In this case they would, evidently, have no natural value.

This was really the case in Athens. The silver mine at Laurion, as all other metal mines, belonged to the state or to its lessees, and they were worked by slaves. The precious metals could not become values from the social dignity of the producers, for the slaves had none. Nor could they become values from the cost of production, for the work of slaves was so cheap that expenses hardly counted at all. Finally, the precious metals as raw materials were, generally, of little use; it was only the few rich who made them into ornaments. Thus we see that gold and silver had no natural value. It was only when they were turned by law into coin that they became generally useful as currency, and this usefulness, given to them by the stamp, made them into a object of value.

Here we have the economic conditions which formed

the inductive material of Aristotle's reasonings. The derivation of *nomisma* from *nomos*, and not from nature, makes now real sense, and is no more a mere etymological makeshift.

* * *

John Locke's participation in economic discussions was as regards theory, a retrogression from Petty to Aristotle and the schoolmen, and as regards practice an adherence to mercantilism at a time when its foundations were being undermined. He wrote on economic subjects in the years 1678 to 1696 (that is, many years after the publication of Petty's *Treatise of Taxes*), and his essays on government against Filmer, whom he confutes with arguments taken from Duns Scotus (social contract) and from jus naturale doctrines; the only new idea of his own is that property, money, inequality arose when man was still in the state of nature, and that government was created by consent and agreement, which then regulated property. He also touches in those two essays on the invention of money by consent and agreement; but his theories of money and value are contained in his two treatises, published in 1692 and 1696, partly against Child's proposal concerning the lowering of the rate of interest by law, and partly against the proposal of Lowndes to raise the denomination of money on the occasion of the great recoinage, 1695–1696.

Locke's theories of money and value are one and all taken from Aristotle's *Politics* and *Ethics* and the commentaries of the schoolmen; his only addition is, as mentioned in a previous chapter, the formulation of the quantity theory. He declares that gold and silver received their value from "fancy and agreement"; money has an "imaginary value," which mankind consented and agreed to put on it. He does not forget to add that money, by its acquired character as a measure of value, became a useful commodity and, like other commodities, subject to fluctuations of value. Further, money being a commodity was made into a pledge, "whereby men were assured to obtain for it valuable things equal to those with which they parted." Even the secondary theory of Aristotle concerning labour as giving value to commodities is taken up by Locke, but not applied to precious metals. He declares that "ninety-nine hundreth of the value of the things" taken from nature are created by labour. Finally, he is in agreement with the schoolmen in regarding money as "a barren thing."

Locke, when leaving the sphere of theory for that of practice, grows into a full-fledged mercantilist. The merchant is placed in the centre of economic life. The manufacturer is hardly mentioned. "Commerce is the only way left us either for riches or subsistence." Riches consist in plenty of money, which can only be obtained by overbalancing exports, by the balance of trade, unless a nation possesses silver mines of its own. Further, "riches do not consist in having more gold and silver, but in having more in proportion than the rest of the world or than our neighbours."

Although money is "a barren thing," interest on it is as lawful as rent, and can be as little limited by law as the rent of land, or the hire of a ship. For they all depend respectively on the proportion between the demand for credit, for land or ships, and the available loan money, arable land, pasture, ships, etc.

Raising the denomination of the coin is a futile business, since "the value of money is determined by its current quantity and the existing trade."[1]

Nicholas Barbon, a contemporary of Locke, is as regards money under the influence of the schoolmen. He strongly defends the opinion that "money has its sole value from the law."[2] He was confirmed in his opinion by the condition of the coin in the ten years prior to the recoinage (1695–1696). Great quantities of coin were clipped on the average by about 40 per cent, so that according to its silver value a pound clipped silver coins was not worth sixty shillings (the rate was 5s. per oz.), but about thirty-six shillings, yet, in buying and selling a clipped shilling bought the same quantity of necessaries as a good shilling, for legally a shilling was a shilling and not less. Or, as Barbon argued six years later: "There can't be a plainer demonstration of this" (that money derives from law) "than by what appears since Parliament has been debating about new coining of money and settling the value of the guineas (1695–1696). For, before this meeting the clipt money passed current as if it were unclipt. But those considerations about calling of it in, presently put a stop to the currancy of it, because by those debates the value of it was made uncertain and no man knew where the loss would fall. As to guineas, before their meetings, guineas went current at 30s., but upon the House of Commons

[1] John Locke, *Works,* 1823, vol. v, pp. 10, 11, 12, 13, 22, 42, 44, 148–149; *Of Civil Government,* §§ 27, 40–43, 46.

[2] Nicholas Barbon, *Discourse on Trade,* 1690, p. 21; *Id., Discourse Concerning Coining,* 1696, p. 26.

voting that they should not exceed 28s., every man presently refused to take them for more."

Mainly for the reason of my desire not to omit any author whom my predecessors regarded as important I mention Rice Vaughan, a member of Gray's Inn, and author of a tract of *Coin and Coinage*. It was written about the year 1640, but published posthumously in 1675. It is largely influenced by Aristotle, Hales, and Malynes. Money is a pledge and a measure "to make the things in exchange equal in value." Value consists in use or delight, or the opinion of them, "but the proportion of that value is wholly governed by scarcity and abundance." There are various kinds of gain on money, "of which the most refined is that of exchange, which is mixed with usury of place and time." The tract contains many historical data on prices and royal revenue in the Middle Ages, and discusses the pros and cons of raising the denomination of money, the circulation of foreign coin in the realm, and deplores the unstable ratio between gold and silver. He pleads for a ratio of 12: 1, "because 12 of all the numbers is most proper for money, being the most clear from fractions" and because this ratio "seems like to square with the conceipt of the alchymists, who call gold *sol* and silver *luna*, whose motions do come near upon the point of 12 for 1" (pp. 9, 10, 18, 36, 43).

The opinion that money is fictitious or that its value is due to consent or agreement of mankind, was last brought forward by David Hume, whom we may call in this respect the last Aristotelian.

* * *

British economic thought from the thirteenth century to the middle of the eighteenth century was predominantly commercial in its character. It exhibits three stages. First, to the middle of the sixteenth century commerce was mainly the export of native raw materials, largely carried on by merchant-strangers and regulated by royal ordinances and theological doctrines as substitutes for economic theories. Next, the English merchants, having grown in strength, ousted the alien competitors, dismissed the theological and old-time economic writers and royal dictators, and took to writing in their own cause themselves. Economic writers, since about 1550, explored all the possibilities and means of foreign trade and later on they began to appreciate also the advantages of working up the native commodities into manufactures. In the third stage, beginning with the Restoration and ending in the middle of the eighteenth century, manufacture increasingly occupied economic thought, gradually laying the foundation—mainly through Petty and the discussions provoked by the protracted conflict between the East India Company and the woollen manufacturers—for the economics of production, thus undermining mercantilism.

The output of economic thought was very considerable. This applies in an increasing degree to the years 1660–1701. The two centuries, 1550–1750, were the nursery of the coming political economists.

Nearly the whole field of human activities for acquiring wealth was sown with doctrinal seeds in the shape of practical rules and reflections, which needed but the trained husbandman to eliminate the obsolescent, to cultivate those capable of growth, and to garner the harvest into an economy.

The century in which the balance of trade was the rule of obtaining treasure demonstrated the role of mercantile capital in enriching the country. It gave to economics the essentials of foreign trade and the elements of credit operations: the value of money lay not in its denomination but in the fineness and weight of its substance; transfer of treasure by bill of exchange; gain on money by arbitrage; mutual influence of quantities of money and commodities on the price of each. But the concepts of wealth and profit bore still the marks of the past bullionist policy: wealth was believed to consist in plenty of money; profit had still its source in mercantile operations, and there was no differentiation between value and price.

The growth of manufactures since the end of the sixteenth century enlarged the scope of economics by the experience that the spring of wealth was not traffic, but production in manufacture and agriculture. The prime cost of production constituted the natural value of commodities: craftsmanship applied to the native raw materials enhanced many times their raw material value, but foreign trade was the only means to convert the values into money or into commodities which we needed. Wealth was seen to consist, not in plenty of coin, but in plenty of commodities, money being one of the commodities, though the most desirable one. This view found general acceptance after the introduction of paper-money. Increase of money, while neutralized by a corresponding rise of prices, was none the less beneficial on account of its stimulating and stirring effect on the springs of wealth.

Profit was found to have its source in the application of craftsmanship to raw materials, or in the surplus of the products which remained after deducting the prime cost of production. Only work of that kind was called productive, while all liberal professions were thought to be unproductive. Craftsmanship was enhanced in its capacity by the division of labour, employment of engines, and more economical organization of the processes of production. But there still remained the old view that the increase of wealth created by the new productive forces could be made available only by means of foreign trade and not by home trade. The latter was thought to be incapable of increasing the wealth of the nation, though since 1690 this view was being seriously challenged.

Labour being the source of wealth, the increase of population was to be encouraged, for the larger the fund of labour power the cheaper each unit. At the same time, it was recognized that the increase of the population was limited by the available means of subsistence. Wages were generally meant to be the bare means of subsistence. The inverse ratio of profit and wages was dimly recognized. At the end of the seventeenth century, when corn was being protected by high duties, *Britannia Languens* complained that such a policy raised the price of victuals and, consequently, the rate of wages, so that manufactured goods were made dear and unsaleable.

Interest on money and its rate were recognized to be a proportionate deduction from profit.

Finally, ever since the beginning of the seventeenth century, the idea was growing in strength that there was inherent in trade a certain natural liberty and self-acting regulator, and that it was therefore best to allow it to operate without state interference, to the mutual benefit of all nations.

The only economic category that still needed to be more fully inquired into was rent. With Petty, rent was the net profit of land cultivation—the surplus of produce after labour and expenses had been deducted, and rent of land a part of that surplus. With Locke and Hume, the payment of rent was the consequence of the inequality of the possession of land: the farmer had to pay rent to the landowner, just as the borrower had to pay as interest to the creditor. Rent was soon going to be a subject of inquiry, for it was thought that, owing to the protection enjoyed by the landed interests, rent was inordinately swollen at the expense of manufacturers and wage earners. Forces were gathering for a conflict between the landed, manufacturing, and commercial interests. The struggle against prohibitions, initiated in the second half of the seventeenth century by the anti-mercantilists, was gradually developing into a conflict between protection and free-trade.

Most of the elements for constructing a system of political economy were thus at hand. It only needed the insight of an intellect capable of synthesis to discern which of the elements promised to combine into an organic whole, and which of them were merely conserved by tradition.

Two Scottish scholars took up the task—Sir James Steuart and Adam Smith. The former, while holding fairly modern views on certain economic categories (price, profit), was, on the whole, a man of the past and quite imbued with the authoritarian spirit of the Stuarts; he looked upon the State as the infallible guide of its erring subjects in all their trading and industrial activities; in this spirit he wrote his *Inquiry into the Principles of Political Oeconomy* (1767). His laborious work fell soon into oblivion. Adam Smith, taking the problems of his time, that is, manufacture and freedom of trade, as a guide, combined all that was vital in the available elements, and rejected all that was moribund. He wrote his *Wealth of Nations* (1776), which became the text-book of students, merchants, and statesmen for a whole century.

INDEX

For Product Safety Concerns and Information please contact our EU
representative GPSR@taylorandfrancis.com
Taylor & Francis Verlag GmbH, Kaufingerstraße 24, 80331 München, Germany

www.ingramcontent.com/pod-product-compliance
Lightning Source LLC
LaVergne TN
LVHW011125300926
849160LV00008B/510
9780415607148